MAHMOUD RASMI

Philosophy for Business Leaders

*Asking Questions, Navigating Uncertainty, and the
Quest for Meaning*

First edition

ISBN: 978-84-09-55950-3

Cover art by Studio Anthony Smyrski
Editing by Telmo Pires
Editing by David Wood

This book was professionally typeset on Reedsy.
Find out more at reedsy.com

"Philosophy is at once the most sublime and the most trivial of human pursuits."

— WILLIAM JAMES

Contents

Introduction: The Philosophical Mindset

From Finance to Philosophy

I never really wanted to study philosophy. In fact, the idea never crossed my mind. At college, after dabbling with a variety of courses that included calculus, organic chemistry, biology, economics, and finance, I decided I wanted to understand what a stock was and the underpinnings of the financial world.

I was mesmerized by all the numbers displayed on big screens, sometimes with weird candle-like figures, squeezed between lines on either side and numbers flaring in red and green every other second.

It looked so fascinating to me that I decided I wanted to be part of that world. At the time, I still had no idea what any of that meant, except that it had to do with finance and the financial markets.

So I decided to major in Business Administration, with a particular focus on banking and finance. This was in the fall of 2007-2008. During that academic year, I enthusiastically signed up for accounting and managerial finance courses, in addition to management, marketing, microeconomics, and macroeconomics, among others. To say that I loved finance would be an understatement.

I was learning new things, gaining insight into how the market forces worked, what a GDP was, product cycles, and marketing techniques. I learned how to read balance sheets and statements of cash flows, conducted cash flow statement analysis with all the weird ratios, explored the relationship between risk and rate of returns, and delved into a great deal of other material that was new, fresh, and completely interesting.

Then one day the world woke up to some disconcerting news. Lehman Brothers declared it was bankrupt, and soon thereafter the repercussions were so vast that the entire world was impacted. It was a global financial crisis.

I had just started learning about financial markets, financial derivatives, security analysis, and portfolio management. I was brimming with questions about the recent developments. Every professor had their unique theory. Reading the news and articles about the unfolding events made things all the more confusing to me. Instead of having answers, I found myself entangled in more questions.

Up until the market collapse, almost everyone exuded confidence in their knowledge and had a highly optimistic outlook on the economy. Then, like a house of cards, it all crumbled. Everything seemed so intricately interconnected and complex that providing a straightforward and simple explanation of the events appeared nearly impossible.

Of course, I was a novice with no prior experience. So I couldn't truly grasp all the information I was absorbing. But it struck me that the sense of certainty and the unwavering confidence financial analysts and economists displayed was abruptly shaken up by a crisis and adversity that only a handful had anticipated.

As banks and financial institutions filed for bankruptcy like falling dominoes, their leadership continued to pile up millions in bonuses. People were losing their jobs, unemployment rates were soaring across the board, many were being evicted from their homes, and the world was shaken by a crisis it wouldn't fully recover from until many years later.

And here I was, pondering numerous questions about finance and how the world operated. I had more queries about dealing with adversity and uncertainty and the potential ethical implications of decisions that affected many people, with seemingly few willing to assume responsibility for their actions.

I wasn't quite sure what to make of it all or where to start in search of answers. However, what I did know was that the finance and economics departments weren't providing a wholly satisfying exploration of these matters.

That was when I considered that perhaps philosophy could be a worthwhile starting point. I had previously taken introductory philosophy and existentialism in literature courses in the Fall of 2007 and Spring of 2008, and I found the subject rather captivating.

Something about philosophy resonated with me. In addition to having a semi-existential crisis, I observed that even though I didn't receive definitive answers to the topics under scrutiny, I was gaining valuable insights into approaching complex issues, posing questions, examining them from various angles, and incorporating historical context into the discussions.

I decided to add a minor in philosophy to my major in banking and finance. Semester in and semester out, I signed up for one or more philosophy courses that dealt with ethics, the theory of knowledge, metaphysics, and modern philosophy, in an attempt to learn a thing or two, gain more insight into philosophical methods of inquiry, and read about the history of philosophy. In the back of my mind, I was hoping to acquire the skills needed to navigate the business world more effectively.

Philosophy opened up a whole new realm to me. What particularly caught my attention was that we were studying individuals who laid the groundwork for fields such as economics, anthropology, and psychology. From David Hume, Adam Smith, John Stuart Mill, Keynes, and Marx, I was slowly learning about the historical and theoretical foundations of the development of economic theory and finance.

However, none of these aspects were covered in my business courses. All we focused on were formulas and calculations. It all appeared quite direct and practical. Facing a financial challenge? No problem, we've got you covered with a formula! Looking to enhance your cash flows? No problem, here's the formula!

Here I was, with one foot in philosophy and the other in business, finance, and economics, and although they appeared complementary to me, a significant gap existed. If I had exclusively pursued philosophy, I would have been missing the technical training in business. Conversely, if I had solely focused on business, I would have lacked the historical depth and critical perspective philosophy provided.

After graduating, I pursued an MA and a PhD in philosophy in Salamanca, Spain, with the intention of returning to teach at my alma mater in Beirut. I believed I could bridge the gap between disciplines and introduce students to the profound world of philosophy. However, I soon received a reality check, and after seven years as a professor, I found myself moving away from academia, with the goal of bringing philosophy to the marketplace. But more on this later.

The Value of Philosophy

"Philosophy is impractical" is a common assertion I frequently encounter and occasionally express myself. There's some truth to it. In modern-day pragmatic terms, philosophy may indeed be useless. Unlike, say, physics or engineering, the results of pursuing philosophy are not immediately noticeable. It does not teach you how to construct a building. That's why it is often perceived as a useless activity. But where does the value of philosophy lie? Does philosophy have any value at all?

In his article "The Value of Philosophy," English philosopher and mathematician Bertrand Russell asserts that in practical terms, philosophy may not be as useful as other fields or subjects. That is because if something doesn't yield measurable results, it is often ignored or discarded.

Russell distinguishes between two kinds of goals that humans pursue: the goods of the body, or physical and material goods that we indulge in, which make our lives easier and more efficient, and the goods of the mind, or intellectual pursuits that aid us in living a better and more meaningful life.

Engaging in philosophy involves tending to the goods of the mind. This pursuit entails exploring new domains, ideas, subjects, and perspectives, but with often uncertain outcomes.

According to Russell, the distinction between philosophy and other disciplines lies in the fact that fields like medicine, law, and science provide mostly definite answers and tangible results, while philosophy encourages us to inquire about the unknown or challenge what we believe we know but remain uncertain about.

As such, the value of philosophy, according to Russell, lies in its uncertainty. Philosophy allows us to venture into the unknown, to ask questions the answers to which are uncertain. It also allows us to avoid the trap of excessive dogmatism, or close-mindedness and bias, in our continuous journey to acquire knowledge and to live a good and more meaningful life.

Either way, this book is not a book about philosophy as a subject.

It is not about what this or that philosopher said in a strict sense, nor is it about why philosophy can be helpful for you or why you should study philosophy in college or at some point in your life.

I frequently come across many articles that focus on the reasons why philosophy is important, why it should be preserved as a subject taught in college, or why you should read philosophy. Then you pick up a philosophy book, and in many instances, you might not understand what the book is about or what the problem it's trying to solve is. Five minutes in, you fall asleep.

On the upside, some philosophy books are a great cure for insomnia. Others, however, might make it worse, especially if you end up thinking too deeply about some of the biggest questions we have not yet been able to answer. For example, what the meaning of it all is, how to live a good life, and how to treat each other in an ethical way.

This book is not about any of the above. I am not going to try to convince you why pursuing a philosophical life would be a great choice to make.

The ancient Greek philosopher Plato thought that pursuing a philosophical life is nothing more than preparing oneself for death.

Another philosopher, Martin Heidegger, thousands of years later would write that to be a human is to be toward death. Meaning that we are aware of what the end of the movie will be like, and our life is simply a continuous striving to make sense of it all, create meaningful friendships, and find ways to produce creatively, be it in art, literature, science, sports, etc.

Despite such a realization, life goes on. School, college, first job, first promotion, friends, partying, partners, more partying, career decisions, life decisions, should I accept this offer? Should I move to a new country? Should I work a bit more and put more effort into this? Should I party more often? Should I have kids? How should I raise them? Should I start my own business? What can I do to improve my lifestyle? How can I make more money? Will the company be able to survive? Should I fire this employee who's not performing well? Should I retire? What are my passions? And the list goes on.

Philosophy as a field is too broad, many different branches tackle diametrically opposing questions. Philosophers often hold differing viewpoints, just like any other business meeting you've been in. The discussions are endless, the topics diverse, and the answers seemingly infinite.

But there's something that many philosophers have in common, and it is this what the book will be about. It is the philosophical mindset that I want to explore with you here.

I will walk you through a handful of frameworks and mental models that eminent philosophers adopted and which made them better problem-solvers, and more effective critical thinkers, and got them better equipped to navigate uncertainty, handle stress, and explore ethical dilemmas.

These frameworks are aimed to be a bit helpful, somewhat actionable, and immediately applicable to your personal and professional life. They are, however, not rigid formulas and may not offer precise solutions to the issues you face, which often depend on a different set of elements and circumstances.

But what this book will provide you with is a set of frameworks that will help you navigate such problems in a fresh perspective, drawing on ancient wisdom, and adapting and applying it to a modern business context.

The seed idea for this book was planted in my head in 2018. I was a university professor, teaching philosophy and cultural studies at two universities in Lebanon, where I am from. I had been teaching philosophy for five years, had slowly been getting fed up with academia, and wanted out because I was gradually getting angry, frustrated, and stressed out.

One day, during the summer of 2019, a few months before Lebanon was hit by an economic crisis and the pandemic, I decided to take a step back and ask myself the following questions: Why was I so stressed? What am I trying to achieve? Where is all this rising anger coming from? What if academic research is not my thing and I should pursue something else? If I were to leave Lebanon, what country would I want to move to? What kind of lifestyle do I want?

Answering all these questions was not an easy task. I had to confront years of decision-making processes and assumptions that I made and admit to all the mistakes I might have committed. Seeking course corrections was essential, but examining oneself and one's life, as the ancient Greek philosopher Socrates insisted, is quite complex.

I did not know what the answers to all these questions were, but I knew I had to change my mindset. I had been too caught up in so many things that I had numerous blind spots. One of them was that I had turned philosophy into a subject I studied, instead of adopting it as a possible tool to reframe problems, shift my perspective, and tackle important issues. It was a wake-up call for me to take a step back, reevaluate, and act accordingly.

Thanks to this realization, I lowered my stress levels over the following months. By asking meaningful questions and using Stoic and existentialist principles to handle stress, I better identified and addressed problems, such as currency devaluation, lost savings due to bank failures, a pandemic lockdown, and the Beirut Port explosion on August 4, 2020.

Philosophy in the Marketplace

In May 2020, I decided to quit my academic job, and through a series of lucky breaks, I managed to start a small business, teaching philosophy to professionals interested in exploring the subject in a non-academic setting. In September 2021, I managed to move to Salamanca, Spain.

Transitioning from academia to the real world was such an eye-opener. Having professionals sign up for my courses instead of undergraduate students made me tweak my teaching approach, the material I curated, and the delivery style.

"Why should I care about what Descartes said?" asked one participant in one of the courses. The question made no sense to me at first. "Because Descartes is important! He is the father of modern philosophy!" is an answer I would have probably given if I were still at university.

But here, the situation was different. These professionals had enrolled in my Introduction to Philosophy course because they wanted to learn something they could apply in their lives, not because they wanted to learn what Descartes said. So I needed to rethink my entire approach.

I had a lot to learn. Not only about marketing, copy, pricing, sales, and content creation but also about who my target audience was, how to make the sessions more practical and relatable, and how to get them to actively participate during the sessions.

To date, I have had over 800 participants enroll in my synchronous courses. I've spoken with many of them, asked for comments and feedback, and through a series of trials and errors over a period of three years, I managed to refine my approach to the courses and workshops

I offer.

The latest workshop I designed, developed, and delivered is called Philosophy for Professionals. It is the result of all the work I have been doing over the past few years, since the day I realized that I needed to reevaluate the path I had taken until then.

I have offered the workshop twice thus far and have had the chance to test the material out and refine it even more. The feedback I got from those enrolled has been positive, and so I decided to write this book to share what I learned along the way, and to explore some of the recurrent issues every business leader, professional, and entrepreneur faces on a daily basis.

As part of my research for the workshop and this book, I conducted interviews with people from diverse personal and professional backgrounds. These interviews offered valuable insights into the challenges they encounter at work and the effective frameworks and tools they use to overcome them.

The interviewees encompassed business leaders, executives, directors, managers, investors, founders, and entrepreneurs across various sectors such as finance, engineering, economics, supply chain, marketing, sales, software development, academia, insurance, consulting, health, and aviation.

Although I haven't included the accounts of all those I interviewed, their valuable perspectives have significantly enriched the content of this book.

Philosophy is Helpful? The Purpose of This Book

Philosophy as a field can be intimidating to those who are not familiar with it. But I invite you to distinguish between academic philosophy, and the philosophy in the marketplace this book is going to be presenting.

So the question is: how can philosophy help you in your life and in the workplace? Did I truly imply that philosophy can be helpful, or even, god forbid, useful? Yes, indeed, I did. This shall be my objective in this book.

Drawing from the insightful discussions I had with the business leaders and entrepreneurs I interviewed for this book, I have reached the following realization: Cultivating a philosophical mindset can be immensely beneficial in equipping individuals to confront and resolve problems, manage stress, navigate uncertainties, and effectively address ethical quandaries.

Much like gyms and other spaces and activities for physical exercise, philosophy serves as a medium for mental exercise. It aids in maintaining mental fitness and preparedness to take action when necessary.

The forms and techniques you learn while lifting at the gym or running on the track provide a guiding framework for improving posture, avoiding injury, and ensuring proper execution of exercises.

However, these forms and techniques may not be directly applicable outside the confines of your training routine. Nonetheless, they are crucial for effectively exercising your muscles and enhancing fitness.

Likewise, philosophy equips you with fundamental forms and techniques to exercise various mental faculties, including the ability to ask better questions for problem identification, reflection on what events are and aren't within your control, consideration of alternative perspectives, and exploration of ethical issues through different frameworks.

When faced with a specific problem, will you sit down and deliberate on the precise formula for asking better questions? Most likely not.

However, cultivating the habit of reflecting on the significance of posing meaningful questions will facilitate problem identification and reframing to explore multiple solutions.

The aim of this book is to create a philosophical gymnasium, not with the intention of becoming professional "bodybuilders," but to practice the art of examining oneself, developing self-awareness, using the Socratic method to ask more meaningful questions, acquiring skills to cope with stress and uncertainty from a Stoic perspective, and gaining insights into the diverse frameworks of ethical reasoning and decision-making.

A Philosophical Mindset: What This Book Offers

The main premise of this book is that a philosophical mindset can help you become a more effective problem solver, handle stress, navigate uncertainty, and tackle ethical dilemmas in a more informed way.

The book is divided into three parts:

1. The Art of Examining Yourself and Questioning Your Assump-

tions

2. Uncertainty, Adversity, and the Quest for Meaning
3. Ethical Decision-Making Frameworks

The parts are structured this way for the following reasons:

The most essential activity that you can undertake as a business leader is to examine yourself. To do that, you have to question your assumptions and deeply rooted beliefs. How can I become a better manager? What is the problem that we are facing? How can we address this problem more efficiently? What decision would be more suitable to solve this problem? Am I making this decision based on assumptions that I have not examined? Is there any evidence that supports the decision I'm making? Should we act immediately, or is this a problem that requires a lot more thought and deep analysis? Could you think of assumptions you take for granted to be true, but you don't really know whether or not they are, in fact, true?

Examining assumptions, and asking more meaningful questions, are important first steps in determining what you know, what you don't know, your points of strength and weakness, identifying a problem, exploring all possible solutions, and finding the most efficient one to solve the problem.

Can you ever be certain about your assumptions, decisions, and plans? How can you make sure you don't get too overwhelmed if you work in a fast-paced environment with many deadlines? When working with a difficult colleague or employee, how can you avoid clashes and ensure a smoother workflow?

Uncertainty surrounds you in your personal and professional life.

Dealing with uncertainty is a tricky matter. Not knowing whether you made the right decision may cause you anxiety and stress. So how can you navigate uncertainty more effectively?

Navigating uncertainty in the business world can be challenging, especially when ethical dilemmas come into play. Consider these scenarios: How do you handle an underperforming employee? What if your personal values clash with the company's values? In tough financial times, do you compromise product quality, knowing it might harm a small portion of your clients? What about accepting gifts or incentives from clients in cultures where such practices are common but might conflict with your company's policies or your country's laws? These situations demand thoughtful reflection and ethical decision-making. In this book, we'll explore philosophical frameworks that can guide you through these complexities, providing you with actionable tools to make well-informed and ethically sound choices in the face of uncertainty.

In this case, you are not only trying to ask yourself more meaningful questions and question your and your colleagues' assumptions while navigating uncertainty, but you are also attempting to address these issues by evaluating different ethical frameworks in the fairest way possible.

Ready to go down the philosophy rabbit hole? Grab a drink, relax, and enjoy the ride.

I

The Art of Examining Yourself and Questioning Your Assumptions

"Great negotiators are able to question the assumptions that the rest of the involved players accept on faith or in arrogance, and thus remain more emotionally open to all possibilities, and more intellectually agile to a fluid situation." — Chris Voss

Part One: Introduction

Shifting Paradigms

In the mid-19th century, when Dr. Ignaz Semmelweis of Hungary proposed that handwashing could significantly reduce mortality rates among newborns at Vienna General Hospital, he was met with unexpected resistance and skepticism from his peers.

Until that time, the dominant medical theory believed that diseases came from 'bad air' or harmful smells from decaying organic material, attributing infections and fatalities to exposure to such tainted atmospheres; the germ theory had not yet been introduced.

Dr. Semmelweis grappled with this problem due to the high mortality rates from childbed fever in one of the hospital's maternity wards.

What he noticed was a bit astounding. The maternity ward with a high mortality rate was staffed with medical doctors and students who went straight to the ward from the dissection rooms, where they conducted autopsies without washing their hands.

The other ward, which had significantly lower mortality rates, was staffed with midwives who had no prior contact with cadavers.

Dr. Semmelweis hypothesized that particles from the corpses might be transferred to the babies, leading to fatal fevers. This problem, he suggested, could likely be solved with handwashing.

To test his theory, he required that medical students and doctors wash their hands with a chlorine solution before attending to births. The results were astonishing. Mortality rates plummeted to ones similar to the other ward staffed by midwives.

You'd probably think that this newly discovered evidence would have convinced the doctors and medical students to adopt a handwashing protocol before attending to births. Unfortunately, this was not the case.

Dr. Semmelweis was met with resistance from the medical community who believed that the miasma theory (contamination through bad air and smells) was true. They also felt insulted by the suggestion that they could be unintentionally causing their patients' deaths.

Dr. Semmelweis felt alienated, and tensions with his colleagues escalated, deepening his sense of frustration. He was eventually admitted to a mental asylum where he ironically died of a septicemia infection.

Years later, his theory would be vindicated by the germs theory proposed by the likes of Louis Pasteur and Joseph Lister. Dr. Semmelweis, an early advocate of handwashing hygiene, is recognized today for his pioneering work in antiseptic procedures.

I chose to begin this part with Dr. Semmelweis' story for several reasons:

First, it underscores the significance of challenging our deeply-held beliefs and our current understanding of the world, even when we consider ourselves authorities in our domain.

Second, the narrative illustrates the often staunch resistance that emerges when established beliefs and assumptions are questioned, even by professionals.

Third, the story paints a vivid picture of the uphill battle involved in altering a worldview we've grown comfortable with, especially when presented with conflicting evidence. This is not a special case, unfortunately.

History shows that new paradigms, scientific, social or economic are not easily and directly adopted. It is rife with many such incidents where, sometimes even against the evidence, people fought hard to maintain the status quo. Within a scientific context, you can check out Thomas Kuhn's book "The Structure of Scientific Revolutions" for more information on the topic.

Fourth, being an authority on a subject doesn't exempt one from introspection; it's vital to continually assess our assumptions.

Lastly, our interpretation of the world, regardless of our expertise, might be heavily influenced by inherent biases that require consistent monitoring and adjustment.

The essential lesson from Dr. Semmelweis' experience is the critical need for a self-reflective approach both individually and collectively, which means periodically revisiting and scrutinizing our decisions, strategies, and assumptions.

Without it, we risk complacency. We may overlook chances for personal and professional development when we rely too heavily on what we think we know. It's essential to occasionally re-evaluate our foundational beliefs and the paradigms we've accepted without question.

In the following discussion, I will explore the significance of challenging our assumptions and how it applies to both our personal and professional realms. As a business leader, similar to an orchestra conductor, or sports team coach, your role involves ensuring the synchronized performance of your company or team. Your responsibilities encompass various aspects such as employee proficiency, client satisfaction, effective internal and external communication, brand consistency, product quality, and achievement of quarterly targets. This can be quite overwhelming.

Between Impostor Syndrome and Self-Assurance

Through my research and interviews with business leaders, a prevailing sense of isolation became apparent. Business leaders often experience mounting pressure to prove their competence and expertise. Implicitly, there's an assumption that they should have all the answers, lest they risk being perceived as inadequate and potentially losing their positions.

In his book "The Hard Thing About Hard Things," venture capitalist Ben Horowitz draws from his CEO experience to underscore a similar sentiment. He presumed other CEOs were confident and certain about their decisions, given their public demeanor. His personal experience was quite the opposite. While he possessed technical knowledge, he was often uncertain about the choices he made as a CEO. He hadn't been trained for this role.

Only later did he realize that many of his seemingly knowledgeable friends also struggled when their companies faced challenges. Impostor syndrome is a genuine phenomenon. It appears that regardless of one's experience, an internal struggle may persist, perpetuating the fear of being exposed.

What triggers this phenomenon? A combination of individual and collective assumptions that we should inherently possess all the answers. This association of knowledge with certainty hampers our willingness to explore things further, beyond our current understanding, potentially leading to stagnation.

If impostor syndrome represents one side of the spectrum, the other extreme can be equally concerning. Much like the CEOs Horowitz mentions, it's problematic to be excessively confident in one's abilities, skills, and knowledge. The situation can become significantly worse when individuals truly believe their expertise is unmatched. It only takes a minor inconvenience for others to realize that their abilities do not align with the high level of confidence they hold in their knowledge and expertise.

The ever-changing sphere of new theories, technologies, and products often goes unnoticed if we fail to critically evaluate our knowledge, beliefs, and assumptions. Consequently, we inadvertently reinforce the notion that expertise should equate to infallible understanding, subjecting us to undue stress and varying degrees of impostor syndrome on the one hand, or self-assurance on the other. What might be one remedy to this rampant problem?

A Philosophical Mindset

Adopting a philosophical mindset can help overcome these challenges by avoiding the trap of extreme self-assurance and overconfidence in what we believe we know. On the other side, it fosters comfort with vulnerability, enabling us to identify our strengths and weaknesses and engage in constructive dialogues that encourage us to question our assumptions, inviting others to do the same. This approach proves particularly valuable during collaborative problem-solving, facilitating the negotiation of solutions while acknowledging the uncertainties with which we all contend.

This part will consist of four chapters, each shedding light on crucial aspects of personal and professional growth. I will be drawing on examples from classical literature, pop culture, and real-life instances gathered from the interviews I've conducted, as well as narratives I've encountered in books and articles.

First, we'll dive into the world of questioning assumptions, drawing inspiration from Socrates and his timeless wisdom. Then, we delve into the art of inquiry, employing the Socratic framework to enhance our critical thinking skills. Next, we'll explore the importance of the trickster mindset in challenging our assumptions and fostering creativity. Last but not least, we'll venture into the realm of changing perspectives and engaging dialogues, drawing inspiration from Plato's "Symposium" and insights from authors like Roger L. Martin.

Chapter One: Examine Yourself: Socrates

A Day at the Court

On the fertile island of Naxos, nestled in the southeast of the Aegean Sea and situated approximately 118 km from Athens, a tragic double homicide unfolds. While carrying out his agricultural duties, a laborer gets drunk and starts fighting with another worker, accidentally killing him.

The landowner decides to wait for the intervention of the relevant authorities, which might span a few days. In the meantime, he confines the perpetrator within a ditch and overlooks attending to him. Soon thereafter, forgotten and without any drink or food, the locked-up aggressor ends up dying.

The landowner's son, angered by his father's actions, heads to court to prosecute him. Upon arriving in the courtyard, he encounters an acquaintance with whom he engages in an interesting exchange.

The above story and the conversation that takes place between the two is from a work of fiction written by the ancient Greek philosopher Plato (427 — 347 BCE); however, it takes inspiration from the historical figures of Socrates (Plato's mentor), and Euthyphro, a self-proclaimed authority on religious matters.

Before the court of King Archon, Euthyphro, the son of the landowner, and Socrates strike up a discussion that starts unremarkably but soon evolves into a spirited conversation.

When you come across someone you recognize at court, you naturally wonder about their purpose, about what brings them there. After exchanging greetings, Socrates and Euthyphro inquire about the reasons behind their respective appearances.

As it turns out, Socrates was summoned on accusations of corrupting the youth, whereas to Socrates' surprise, Euthyphro was prosecuting his father for negligent murder.

Euthyphro boasts about his actions, affirming that he is in the right because he is well-versed in matters of holiness, piety, right, and wrong.

Yet, the irony is that the established law at the time would allow only the victim's relatives to file a lawsuit and press charges against the culprits.

This detail seems to have eluded Euthyphro's attention, as he proudly proclaimed that he knew precisely what he was doing by prosecuting his father, and according to him, it was indeed a pious (holy, good) deed. This doesn't mean that he should have refrained from prosecuting his father, who had obviously committed manslaughter. If Euthyphro was genuinely interested in bringing his father to court, there were other more viable options available, such as reaching out to one of the victim's relatives.

I'll spare you the details of the dialogue. Socrates, not fully convinced, initiates a series of questions for Euthyphro to unravel the motives behind his decision. Is Euthyphro truly knowledgeable about the right course of action, and if so, what can one learn from such an authority on the topic, or is there another underlying reason?

Socrates prompts Euthyphro to define piety because, at first glance, he appears well-acquainted with the subject.

Of course, Euthyphro struggles to offer a clear definition, he mixes up definitions and examples, and can't really come up with a satisfying answer. After several rounds of exchange, he becomes annoyed and quickly takes off, forgetting about why he was at court in the first place, bidding Socrates farewell and saying the following: *"Another time, Socrates; right now I have an urgent engagement somewhere, and it's time for me to go."*

Overconfidence In Our Beliefs and Knowledge

I've taught this dialogue many times, more than I could possibly recall, both in my Introduction to Philosophy and Ethics courses. It usually serves as an accessible introduction to both Plato and Socrates, offering a glimpse into Socrates' teachings and the Socratic method.

This method is a framework employing open-ended probing questions to unveil concealed assumptions, ignite critical thinking, foster insightful conversations, and cultivate a deeper understanding of oneself and grasp of the subject under scrutiny.

The Socratic method was initially popularized by Socrates' student, Plato, and formed the bedrock of his educational approach. Today, this framework finds relevance across diverse sectors including education, research, law, therapy & counseling, medicine, and business and leadership training. We will explore the method in more detail in the next chapter.

While considering the dialogue during my research for this book, I realized that I had overlooked a crucial aspect concerning the character of Euthyphro. He appears to epitomize an individual who radiates unwavering confidence in their knowledge, beliefs, and capabilities, yet conspicuously lacks the awareness, and more significantly, self-awareness required to step back and scrutinize themselves, their assumptions, and the ramifications of their actions.

Just like Euthyphro, we at times fall into the trap of believing we know more than we actually do. This overconfidence often emerges before exams, projects, lectures, teamwork, business endeavors, or even when steering a company. So let's dig a bit deeper into what self-awareness is before going back to Socrates.

Self-awareness

Research[1] reveals a significant gap between our self-assessment and external evaluations. This divide, as outlined by David Dunning, stems from an astounding skill deficit in cultivating self-awareness and conducting accurate self-evaluation.

Over the past 50 years, the significance of self-awareness has grown within the area of management. Extensive research has examined the relationship between self-awareness and performance. Can under-

---

[1]   https://journals.sagepub.com/doi/10.1111/1467-8721.01235

standing ourselves better genuinely enhance performance, improve communication, sharpen moral judgment, and foster empathy? Yes, and this doesn't require elaborate studies to demonstrate.

Self-awareness empowers you to pinpoint your strengths and weaknesses, understand your values and preferences, and identify the areas where growth and improvement are needed. It's the compass guiding you towards personal development and reaching your best potential.

Defining this elusive concept poses some challenges. In her book "Insight: Why We're Not as Self-Aware as We Think, and How Seeing Ourselves Clearly Helps Us Succeed at Work and in Life," Tasha Eurich delves into the current state of self-awareness research.

Eurich's observation exposes the fragmented nature of the available studies, primarily arising from the lack of consensus on a clear definition. While some equate self-awareness with self-consciousness, others emphasize its introspective nature, and still others center on the gap between our self-perception and how we are perceived by others.

The absence of a clear definition makes it harder to understand self-awareness and how we can develop and leverage it for personal and professional growth. Eurich's research proposes seven distinct insights possessed by those with heightened self-awareness. These insights distinguish them from the unaware. According to Eurich, self-aware individuals: *"understood their values, passions, aspirations, fit, patterns, reactions, and impact."*

Eurich defines self-awareness as *"The will and the skill to understand who we are, including our values, patterns, and impact on others (internal self-awareness), and how others see us (external self-awareness)."*

What I like about the definition is that it recognizes the importance of both: internal self-awareness (how we see ourselves), and external self-awareness (how others see us.) This is essential because introspection is necessary but not sufficient.

Think back to a college moment when you were completely confident in your grasp of biology or physics, only to realize your understanding fell short when the exam results turned out to be disappointing.

What was your initial response? Did you blame the difficulty of the exam, the professor's inadequate explanation, or the grudge he may have held against the students? Or did you reflect on your knowledge and consider improvement?

Introspection alone falls short here. Besides internal reflection, seeking peer feedback and consulting the professor can uncover blind spots and areas that escaped your notice.

Using relatable examples like these enables us to explore the interplay between self-perception and external feedback. This dynamic helps us identify room for growth, challenge assumptions, and enhance personal and professional development.

Here's another example. Frank thinks he's an incredibly funny stand-up comedian. He genuinely believes this and can't help but laugh at his own jokes. After laboring over his act in the confines of his home office, dedicating an entire year to crafting a great set, he finally took the stage at the comedy store. After ten minutes into the show, Frank realized that no one had been laughing. He placed the blame on the audience and left midway. Following presentations in five different venues without receiving a single laugh, Frank eventually came to the realization that perhaps the crowd wasn't the issue.

Of course, I'm exaggerating and abstracting things a bit for the purpose of illustrating the point. But you get the gist. Although cultivating and honing our introspective skills is important, it's equally crucial to possess external self-awareness rooted in how others perceive us.

While it's simple to explore self-awareness in comedy or education, things can get more complicated in areas like our work and personal lives. This is because the feedback loop becomes tricky, choices are more varied, and decisions often lack clear right or wrong answers.

What makes it even trickier is that in our jobs, we might easily fall into the trap of thinking that we are experts. Expertise bias can hinder growth as it gradually narrows our openness to feedback and halts the pursuit of ongoing improvement, potentially resulting in stagnation and numerous mistakes.

The Self-awareness Paradox

Research[2] indicates that we are not as self-aware as we think we are at work. Insufficient self-awareness inevitably impacts a team's performance, rendering it less effective in terms of collaboration, communication, and coordination.

The situation worsens as those with inadequate self-awareness tend to overestimate their contributions. Team tension emerges, leading to discord and inefficiency, thereby complicating project completion, goal achievement, and problem-solving.

---

[2] https://hbr.org/2015/03/research-were-not-very-self-aware-especially-at-work

If this is the case in the workplace, I don't even want to imagine how it is in our daily lives. Have you ever been in a meeting, a group hangout, dinner with friends, or a public gathering with someone who is simply unaware of their surroundings or the consequences of their actions? What if that person is you? How can you snap out of such a state and start working on improving your self, situational, and contextual awareness?

The issue and paradox stem from the fact that we not only lack self-awareness but are also unaware of the potential lack of it. This is what puzzled researchers, including David Dunning in the previously mentioned study.

The primary challenge Dunning and his colleagues encountered is that the lack of awareness of one's incompetence doesn't stop there; the curse is twofold because some individuals also lack the ability to recognize their own incompetence. Consequently, we encounter incompetent people who remain blissfully unaware while simultaneously overestimating their level of competence.

The question that arises is the following: considering that self-awareness is vital for personal and professional growth, empathy, active and attentive listening, receptivity to feedback, pursuit of development, and enhanced problem-solving, what are some of the best ways to develop and improve this skill? How can we avoid being the Euthyphro in our personal and professional lives?

To achieve this, we must initially identify the potential obstacles that could hinder us from attaining awareness.

These encompass:

- **Lack of self-reflection:** Failure to engage in introspective exercises to identify your values, principles, possible strengths, and weaknesses.
- **Fear of change:** Resistance to changes in your worldview, thoughts, and beliefs due to a preference for the familiar and a reluctance to explore the unknown.
- **Avoidance of discomfort:** Evading uncomfortable feelings and situations that might induce unease, such as receiving feedback or interacting with individuals holding differing opinions.
- **Closed-mindedness:** Assuming that your beliefs and thoughts are already true, and therefore disregarding the need for further exploration or testing by engaging with others.
- **Fear of and/or lack of feedback:** Absence of more experienced individuals, mentors, or coaches who could provide valuable feedback, or avoiding feedback at all costs due to an inability to handle discomfort, skepticism about the value of comments, or uncertainty about its worth.
- **Contentment with the status quo:** Finding satisfaction with the current state of affairs, adhering to the saying "ignorance is bliss."

Know yourself

The adage "Know thyself," which was inscribed on the entrance of the Apollo Temple at Delphi in ancient Greece, should hardly be a surprise to us. Knowing yourself is an essential initial step before seeking external guidance, whether it's from the Oracle at Delphi, a supervisor, manager, director, or anyone else. Without proper introspection to understand yourself, it could become challenging to fully appreciate the value of the information you're receiving.

But what are some practical steps we can take to overcome the

obstacles mentioned earlier?

- **Self-awareness requires knowledge:** knowledge of ourselves, others, and the world.
- To seek and continuously strive to improve our knowledge requires that we **maintain a curious mindset and a willingness to continuously learn**, revise, adapt, and improve our assumptions.
- A curious mindset without the **willingness to question our assumptions** is only going to make us more stubborn, less open to growth, and less exposed to other perspectives.
- In order to be willing to question our assumptions, a lot of work has to be done: we need to **learn how to ask questions, we need to listen attentively to others,** and we ought to be willing to do the hard work to seek out better outcomes, and also be willing and open to feedback.
- In other words, it's an ongoing feedback process. It involves constant self-examination, curiosity, continuous learning, and development. It requires refining our beliefs and worldviews, gaining new experiences, engaging in dialogue with others, honing our skills, improving our listening, empathy, and collaboration skills, and learning how to inquire, negotiate, and be open to feedback.

The 'know thyself,' 'self-awareness,' and lack of awareness about one's incompetence paradox persists. We understand the significance of introspection and external self-awareness, along with the importance of asking questions. But how can we be certain that we are progressing toward clearer self-knowledge and overall growth? What impact does self-examination truly have? And how can it prove beneficial in both our personal and professional lives?

To address these questions, we ought to delve deeper into Socrates' teachings by briefly examining who Socrates was and why he is significant. Then, I'll outline the Socratic method that will assist you in:

- Understanding the significance of examining your personal and professional lives.
- Being more receptive to questioning your assumptions, beliefs, and worldviews.
- Refining the questions you pose to concentrate on more meaningful aspects during conversations.
- Cultivating more thoughtful interactions with others.
- Prioritizing problem-solving over winning arguments.
- Applying the Socratic method's principles to the challenges you face in the workplace.

"The unexamined life is a life not worth living." — Socrates

Euthyphro's lack of self-awareness and failure to examine his assumptions was clear in how he handled the conversation with Socrates. He was vexed and practically ran away from the court forgetting why he was there to begin with.

Socrates, on the other hand, was there for a more serious issue. He was accused of corrupting the youth, creating new gods, and ultimately, he was facing the death penalty.

In modern-day business terms, think about whistleblowers and people who wrestled against corporate giants and found it difficult to make their case. I don't want to mention any names because this can derail the conversation and shift the focus to whether or not these people are heroes. I don't even want to explore whether or not Socrates was one. But his story is interesting nonetheless.

Much like the Hungarian gynecologist Dr. Semmelweis, mentioned earlier, who got ostracized for questioning the established medical norms, Socrates was prosecuted for fostering critical thinking and encouraging Athenian youth to ask questions, examine their lives, and reevaluate the established societal norms.

I chose to start with Dr. Semmelweis' story because it's more similar to Socrates' story than one might initially imagine. Socrates' mother was a midwife. Inspired by her, Socrates referred to himself as a midwife of ideas (maieusis).

A pioneering philosopher, mentor, coach, and educator, Socrates departed from the common norms of his time. His method did not adhere to the conventional processes of imparting knowledge and sharing wisdom with students, focusing solely on knowledge transmission.

Instead, he firmly believed in the importance of asking guided, open-ended questions and engaging in thoughtful conversations to dissect specific topics to have a more well-rounded grasp of them.

This approach nurtured self-examination and introspection, which enabled a deeper understanding of the issues at hand and a more holistic awareness of how they related to and applied in his students' personal, social, and professional lives.

In educational terms, Socrates was an early proponent of what is today known as the 'generation effect'. The premise of this learning approach is that when students encounter obstacles and difficult problems and are compelled to devise solutions independently, even in the face of failure, they ultimately acquire a deeper comprehension of the subject at hand compared to those who receive hints.

The rationale behind this concept, as explained by David Epstein in his book "Range," is that when we are provided with hints regarding how to solve a specific problem, we tend to incorporate and replicate a certain pattern for solving it based on prior experiences. Epstein highlights the paradox underpinning these two approaches.

In a traditional setting, the employed methods sacrifice long-term benefits for short-term successful performance, whereas the "generation effect" method trades short-term performance for more enduring long-term advantages. Epstein attributes the development of such an unorthodox method to Socrates.

> "Socrates was apparently on to something when he forced pupils to generate answers rather than bestowing them. It requires the learner to intentionally sacrifice current performance for future benefit."

During his free time, Socrates frequented the marketplace (agora) in Athens and engaged in conversations with passersby, discussing a wide array of topics, including love, justice, piety, the concept of the good, and the optimal way to lead one's life. In modern terms, think also about optimal ways to become more effective leaders, managers, professionals, athletes, etc.

We've previously witnessed a brief example of Socrates' interactions through the exchange with Euthyphro. You might be thinking to yourself, what an annoying little twat this Socrates fellow was. To some extent, some people did view him this way and he even proudly nicknamed himself "gadfly."

Socrates would likely have embraced this label as his social media handle. Imagine encountering him while you're going about your business, only to find yourself questioned about the definitions of piety, goodness, justice, love, or the best diet and exercise regimen, tips to create a superb YouTube video, and hold an effective meeting.

Just as a coin has two opposing sides, Socrates not only had detractors, but he also garnered a substantial following — people who began to question their assumptions, evaluate their lives, and scrutinize the norms and daily routines of Athens and neighboring city-states.

As the movement gained momentum and more individuals engaged in thoughtful dialogues and critical examinations of the status quo, those in positions of power grew increasingly irritated.

The consequence? Socrates faced charges of corrupting the youth and introducing new gods. As a result, he received a death sentence. Despite being offered the option to leave Athens for exile elsewhere, he ultimately chose to embrace his fate and drank the poison.

It's worth noting that he didn't advocate any particular philosophical system or present novel theories, unlike Dr. Semmelweis. Instead, he simply posed questions, facilitated dialogues, and encouraged people to scrutinize their lives. As he famously stated, *"The unexamined life is not worth living."*

We possess limited knowledge about Socrates' life because he deliberately refrained from writing anything down. Our understanding of him is derived from the fictionalized dialogues penned by his student Plato, who was committed to preserving Socrates' teachings for future generations. Plato believed that Socrates was unjustly condemned to death and that the charges against him lacked substance and were unfounded.

In Plato's dialogue, "The Apology," the hearing and defense of Socrates are portrayed, wherein Socrates explains that his wisdom stems from recognizing his own ignorance. He emphasizes that continuous self-examination is crucial for leading a good life.

> "There is another thing: - young men of the richer classes, who have not much to do, come about me of their own accord.
> They like to hear the pretenders examined, and they often imitate me and examine others themselves.
> There are plenty of persons, as they soon enough discover, who think that they know something, but really know little or nothing: and then those who are examined by them instead of being angry with themselves are angry with me.
> "This confounded Socrates", they say; this villainous mis-leader of youth!
> And then if somebody asks them, why, what evil does he practice or teach?
> They do not know, and cannot tell." — Excerpt of Socrates' defense speech from The Apology by Plato

Socrates' statement is quite interesting: when those who are being examined recognize their ignorance of topics they assumed to be experts in, they don't direct their frustration inward or endeavor to enhance their understanding of the matter; instead, their anger is directed at Socrates.

This reaction is rather common. We've all found ourselves in similar situations at some point, and it's likely that we frequently experience these emotions when our assumptions and beliefs are questioned. Yet, what might trigger this reaction? One plausible explanation may lie in what Will Storr terms the theory of control.

We Are Wired to Control Things Around Us

In his book "The Science of Storytelling" Will Storr dives into some core questions about what makes a story truly captivating: What turns a story into a must-read? How can we tell the difference between a well-crafted tale and a lackluster one? What ingredients weave together to form a skillfully narrated story?

Storr digs deep into the layers of narrative, carefully examining each aspect to uncover its true essence. Here are some observations he makes:

1. Deep down, our minds yearn to make sense of our world. We do this by naming things, creating stories, and using storytelling to explain how everything fits together – from societal norms to who we are and how we relate to our environment. This is what Storr calls the **theory of control**. The stories we craft about ourselves and the world based on our deeply held beliefs are often flawed.
2. Those moments when our beliefs are challenged can lead to personal growth. Embracing change allows us to break free from narrow thinking and extremism.

3. Think of change as an invitation to embark on an adventure. Embracing uncertainty, questioning assumptions, testing new hypotheses, and exploring new horizons all contribute to our personal and collective growth.

4. These very elements are what make stories like Homer's "Odyssey", and J.R.R. Tolkien's "The Hobbit" or movies like "Star Wars," "The Matrix" and "The Truman Show" so captivating. Yet, our resistance to change often comes from wanting to stay in our comfort zone. However, adapting thoughtfully and flexibly can lead to significant growth, much like physical exercise enhances our physical resilience.

Throughout history, our need for certainty and control has given us a sense of security. This need drove early societies to create stories and myths about the world's origins and complexities. Similarly, giving names to things is a way for us to assert our dominance over the world. It's not just about sorting things efficiently; it's about making the unfamiliar familiar.

We're essentially trying to "tame" our environment and the world, much like how we categorize ourselves and people into labels – liberal, conservative, communist, bitcoin enthusiast – to make approaching and interacting with others simpler.

This process, though, often leaves little room for complexity or understanding nuance. It's rooted in assumptions about others and ourselves, fueling dogmatic, or rigid and stubborn, thinking.

We react to the world based on our beliefs, forming a narrative that shapes our perspective and often leads us to polarized views on important issues. We tend to gravitate toward like-minded individuals, closing ourselves off from opposing viewpoints. But why? It's because we've already labeled them as the "opposition."

Ben Horowitz draws on his journey through self-discovery to highlight this point. Raised in a household that staunchly believed capitalism was evil, he found himself later swinging to the opposite extreme of embracing it wholeheartedly. He eventually found a middle ground. He realized that both sides held valid points. Extremes like unchecked capitalism and total communism each come with their dangers.

The real world isn't black and white; it's a spectrum of complexity. Horowitz's transformation came through questioning his assumptions, seeking diverse perspectives, engaging in meaningful conversations, and truly listening to differing viewpoints. His experience speaks volumes about the potential for growth when we break free from rigid beliefs and embrace the multifaceted reality that business leaders face daily. In "The Hard Things About Hard Things," Horowitz affirms:

> "Until you make the effort to get to know someone or something, you don't know anything. There are no shortcuts to knowledge, especially knowledge gained from personal experience. Following conventional wisdom and relying on shortcuts can be worse than knowing nothing at all."

This quote echoes and succinctly encapsulates the teachings of Socrates. **Do you think you know something really well? Think again. Do you think you know someone really well? Think again.**

Thinking again requires some level of self-awareness, a willingness to question one's own assumptions, a drive to dialogue with others, and the courage to ask oneself and others meaningful questions.

If we are somehow inherently wired to make sense of ourselves, the world, our environment, and the people around us by exerting a certain degree of control, **which is often times flawed**, and constructing narratives about ourselves, others, and the world, what steps can we take to become more receptive to questioning our beliefs and assumptions, honing our concepts, and fostering personal growth? If internal and external self-awareness is essential to the whole process, how can we cultivate this skill so as to work on becoming better versions of ourselves in our personal and professional lives?

I don't really have any direct answer to these questions. Self-awareness as a concept is quite paradoxical as we have already discussed. It's fairly easy to assume that we are self-aware. It's even easier to accuse others of lacking self-awareness.

Chances are you've done that several times over the course of your life. Maybe you thought a friend, a colleague, or a boss of yours lacked self-awareness. But does announcing to ourselves and others that we are now self-aware make us so? How do we know that we are on the right track? And in what way does cultivating self-knowledge and self-awareness make us better and more effective communicators, team players, and problem solvers?

All these questions piling up are meant to get you to think about this issue further and perhaps consider it from different angles. The angle I'm going to be zooming in on involves an exploration of the relationship between our desire for control in general, our inherent disposition to create narratives, and our need to fit in and be accepted.

Miranda & Peter: A Spectrum

Miranda Priestly proves herself a tough and demanding boss, holding the position of editor-in-chief at the popular fashion magazine, Runway. Her proficiency is evident; she possesses impressive skills, an extensive grasp of the fashion industry, and a strong sense of aesthetics. Her demanding demeanor may, in part, be responsible for her effectiveness, although she also inclines toward authoritarian tendencies.

Miranda's self-awareness seems limited to the confines of her office, which serves as the epicenter of the world revolving around her. She also has enough personal problems too. But for the sake of this example, I will only focus on her actions as a boss. Her authoritative approach can be quite challenging to navigate. So much so, within fashion and magazine circles, it's widely recognized that enduring a year as her assistant signifies exceptional ability.

The underlying assumption is that such an experience presents numerous chances to learn how to handle and adapt to the high-pressure, cutthroat environment inherent in working alongside Miranda.

You might probably already know that Miranda Priestly is a fictional character from the novel "The Devil Wears Prada," written by Lauren Weisberger. It was subsequently adapted into a movie, in which Meryl Streep portrays the character of Miranda.

While we can explore Miranda's character from different angles, I will be focusing on the aspects that highlight the absence of self-awareness. But before we explore this further, let's go over another example first.

Meet Peter Gibbons, a model employee in a corporate environment. Employed as an office worker at Initech, Peter strives to seamlessly fit into and conform to office culture. Despite contending with redundant bureaucracy and frequent, irrational requests from his boss, he perseveres, albeit with mounting frustration. In the end, securing his boss's approval remains a necessity if he wishes to advance within the company.

Peter's morale hit rock bottom as he set aside his personal interests, family, and friends to embrace an established societal norm that prioritized corporate culture and career advancement above all else.

You might be familiar with this employee archetype – someone who's willing to set aside their authentic self in pursuit of professional success. Alternatively, you might recall Peter, a fictional character from the 1999 film "Office Space," directed by Mike Judge.

During the movie, Peter undergoes a radical transformation, gradually becoming more self-aware about what his interests are, and slowly working on improving his life, cultivating friendships and relation-ships, and seeking more meaning in what he does.

But that detail doesn't hold much significance for us at the moment, because without undergoing any transformation or change, Peter's character stands on the opposite side of the self-awareness spectrum. He personifies someone who doesn't know what he wants, and in his struggle to fit in, ends up suppressing his personality, interests, and the pursuit of a more authentic life in the hope of finding greater acceptance within a certain tribe, in this case, his boss and the corporate environment.

Based on these two examples, we can establish a spectrum with two extremes to analyze the relationship between our inherent desire for control, the importance of cultivating self-awareness, and how questioning our assumptions and shifting our perspectives could help us balance the two effectively.

On one end of the spectrum, there's Amanda Priestly, whose complete lack of internal and external self-awareness, but an extreme desire for control, manifests through her imposing authoritative style. She doesn't care how, when, or in what way the employees ought to get something done; her orders and requests have to be met at all costs.

This becomes more salient in the movie when she asks her new assistant, Andy (played by Anne Hathaway), to find a way to be back home in time for her to attend her daughters' recital, despite the adverse weather conditions and flight cancellations.

Andy obviously fails to meet this impossible request, which makes a disappointed Miranda consider firing her unless she manages to get her hands on a copy of the unpublished Harry Potter manuscript.

Miranda's desire for control and lack of awareness and empathy made her an authoritarian and insufferable boss.

On the other extreme, we encounter Peter Gibbons, who nearly relinquished the desire for control and lacked both external and internal self-awareness, preventing him from understanding who he was or what gave meaning to his life.

Consequently, Peter almost transformed into a puppet manipulated by his boss and all the other managers and directors who required him to act in a specific manner, reprimanded him when he didn't comply, and even asked him to exert additional effort and work overtime.

The question that arises is as follows: How can we strike a balance between our innate desire for certainty, comfort, and control, while also cultivating heightened self-awareness, questioning our assumptions, seeking growth, pursuing an authentic existence, and avoiding the pitfalls of becoming authoritarian or conformist?

I will propose the following steps which will be discussed in detail in the following chapters.

The aspiration to express oneself authentically while embracing growth and questioning assumptions presents a challenge. One potential framework involves embracing multiple dimensions:

1. **Engaging the Socratic Method:** By actively asking probing questions, shifting perspectives, engaging with different viewpoints, and exposing ourselves to diverse experiences, we increase our internal and external self-awareness.

2. **Embracing a Trickster Attitude:** By adopting a trickster attitude, such as Prometheus or Hermes, we become better disposed to explore uncharted paths, challenge norms, and test out new ideas. This approach encourages us to cultivate a mindset of continuous exploration.

3. **Focusing on solving problems rather than winning debates:** While winning arguments and debates may sometimes be important, a more effective way to grow personally and professionally is to seek to solve problems. This fosters a more collaborative approach and encourages a more innovative and creative output.

Chapter Two: The Socratic Framework of Inquiry

Attentive Listening and the Discomfort of Feedback

In a keynote speech[3] given at the University of Kansas, aerospace engineer and former CEO of Boeing and Ford, Alan Mulally, shared one of the many insights he gained during his career. His first job was as an airplane design engineer at Boeing. He performed so well that they promoted him to manage a team of one employee who quit shortly afterward.

Disheartening as this was, Alan reached out to the employee to seek feedback and understand the reason for the departure. The employee pointed out that Alan was attempting to make him work in a certain way—namely, the way Alan did things—instead of aiding him in exploring his own skills and utilizing them to contribute to the company's success.

During the speech, Alan explained his epiphany: *"I had been trying to make my employee do things exactly the way that I did, instead of helping*

---

3   https://youtu.be/WtqU1ekd9Qg

him discover and develop his unique talents to support the business and the needs of the company. Over time, I learned that the most effective managing leaders connect people to the compelling vision of the enterprise in a way that benefits the individual and benefits the organization."

I became aware of the keynote speech through Tasha Eurich, who recounts this story fully in her book "Insight." I believe this anecdote effectively highlights the significance of awareness in general, self-awareness specifically, and the importance of asking questions, challenging assumptions, and seeking feedback.

Alan must have assumed he was an excellent manager solely because of his promotion. The reaction of his employee (Mike, according to Tasha Eurich) indicated otherwise. Rather than opting to ignore Mike's decision to quit and dismiss it as anecdotal, or placing blame on his potential incompetence, possible lack of awareness, or accusing him of being unskilled or ignorant about what he was doing, Alan chose to view himself through the lens of Mike's departure. He inquired, "What aspects of my behavior prompted your departure?" Mike's response revealed that Alan's micromanagement was insufferable, with expectations for Mike to mimic and replicate his behavior.

Alan listened attentively to Mike's feedback, absorbed it, processed it, and decided to work on himself—his management approach and his interactions with teammates. This effort led to his becoming a more successful leader, evident in his accomplished track record as CEO of Boeing and later Ford, guiding them through challenging periods. The lesson? Continuously examine yourself, cultivate and maintain a curious mindset, embrace feedback openly, and assist employees in uncovering and nurturing their skills, rather than anticipating them to replicate one's individual style, knowledge, and skills.

A Catalyst for Change, The Hero's Journey, and Catharsis

The intricate aspect of cultivating the awareness and willingness to delve into self-examination and self-understanding is that we frequently require a catalyst to push us into motion. This impetus can be instigated by external events, spanning from minor, inconsequential encounters or conversations to more serious or even tragic events, such as the loss of a loved one.

This action or event is, indeed, what Will Storr contends forms a captivating narrative in storytelling. Every gripping story begins with an action that initiates transformation. This action directly or indirectly challenges the protagonist's perspective, belief system, and assumptions, setting in motion a gradual process of growth and refinement through a sequence of events.

This is usually known as 'the hero's journey' discussed in depth by Joseph Campbell. Think, for example, Hercules, Odysseus, Rocky, Spider-Man, Harry Potter, etc. The reason why we like these stories is not only because we identify with the protagonist, but we vicariously live through them.

Of course, it's often easier to relate to a protagonist and empathize with their hardships, struggles, and catalysts for growth when these experiences are happening to them rather than us. Greek philosopher Aristotle explains that this is because we can undergo a catharsis of emotions through their journey.

Think of catharsis as the flushing and purification of our emotions that we vicariously experience as we witness a character's journey through challenges and triumphs. By empathizing with a character's emotions, we can turn inward to process our own feelings, fears, and hopes in a safe manner, especially when the stakes are low. This connection allows us to introspect and explore our desires and vulnerabilities without any immediate consequences.

But when we are called to an adventure in real life, things don't always unfold as they do in the movies. Why? Achieving self-awareness, scrutinizing ourselves, challenging our assumptions, and balancing our need for control and certainty with the ambiguity and complexity of the unknown is an exceedingly challenging feat. It's not easy to look deep within ourselves and admit that we are wrong, or that despite assuming that we are experts on a certain topic there's a lot more to learn.

That's why Socrates exclaimed that when he invited his interlocutors to examine their assumptions they got angry at him instead of at themselves when they realized that they didn't really know about a certain topic as much as they assumed they did.

Philosophy: Love of Wisdom

As we have previously mentioned, Socrates believed that an unexamined life is not worth living. This perspective stems from the idea that in order to lead a good and fulfilling life, we must comprehend what constitutes such a life and how to attain it. The question arises: How can we truly understand what it means to lead a good life? The answer lies in our willingness to introspect and engage in thoughtful dialogues with others.

Delving into the concept of a good life necessitates a thorough examination of how we should coexist as a society, what defines a harmonious societal structure, the elements of effective governance, and the collective progress required to contribute to the greater good.

This involves tackling challenges such as disease prevention, personal and communal nurturing, and imparting virtuous values to future generations. For Socrates and Plato, this form of philosophical inquiry embodies the essence of philosophical activity.

The term "philosophy" originates from the Greek words "philos" (loving) and "sophos" (wisdom), forming "love of wisdom." In ancient Greece, philosophy was viewed as a way of life. To be a philosopher meant embracing the pursuit of truth and knowledge to lead a wise and meaningful existence. The ultimate objective of this wisdom was to prepare oneself for the inevitability of death.

We can extrapolate this approach to the business world, though. What does a good leader look like? What are some of the important elements to ensure a harmonious, effective, well-functioning company? What can we do to ensure that employees are happy and are provided with the right environment and tools to develop their skills, grow, and become more effective problem solvers and communicators?

A more conventional approach would resemble Alan Mulally's initial method, which ultimately pushed his only employee to resign. This approach involved a deficiency in self-awareness, combined with an overwhelming desire for control. It manifested in the form of micromanagement and the anticipation that employees replicate tasks exactly as the supervisor does. This mode of operation is also mirrored in the teaching techniques of some educators, educational systems, parents, coaches, and more.

The underlying assumption is that there exists knowledge to be transferred to students, and the students must memorize and reproduce this knowledge to grasp and internalize the material. What happens is that often times we think we know something because we simply learned it by heart, but upon a closer examination, we realize that we lack a proper understanding because we either lack depth, perspective, or the proper experience to share our knowledge of this subject.

Socrates embraced a different approach that saw trainees and students not as receptacles for knowledge, but as active agents in the reception of and subsequent creation of knowledge. Something akin to the 'generation effect' mentioned earlier.

I want to take a moment here to stress that this does not mean that students are going to be generating knowledge from scratch. Of course, in order to learn a mathematical concept, you have to be exposed to it first. But, this is not a sufficient indicator that we actually grasped the concept.

I would invite you to recall how confident you were about your understanding of a certain mathematical topic only to find out that you didn't really get it as soon as you attempted to solve the exercises for homework.

That's precisely what Socrates did. He frequented the marketplace with a laidback, almost trickster demeanor, and asked people about a particular topic to examine it in more depth.

"What is justice? What is virtue? What is love?" These broad questions about the definitions of highly abstract concepts aimed to challenge his interlocutors, who often professed to possess more knowledge about the subject than they actually had.

Consequently, the dynamic that shaped the Socratic dialogue consisted of initial attempts to address the question, which were then met with more probing questions (often accompanied by a sarcastic undertone), without necessarily arriving at a definitive answer, if one was reached at all.

Socratic Method

This came to be known as the Socratic dialectic, akin to a dialogue. Ultimately, the goal of such an exercise was not so much to find a clear definition of the concept in question, but to establish a rapport that assisted the interlocutors and the listening audience in developing a mechanism for attaining a deeper understanding of the range of ethical, social, and metaphysical subjects with which humans typically grapple. Socrates would merely scratch the surface, using pertinent questions to challenge prevailing perspectives and dogmas.

The aim of the Socratic method isn't primarily to discover a conclusive answer to challenging questions. Instead, it serves as a technique that:

1. Promotes independent thinking.
2. Fosters curiosity.
3. Challenges our deeply rooted assumptions and beliefs.
4. Encourages thoughtful exchanges.
5. Helps us appreciate the complexity of the world around us.
6. Allows us to gain a deeper understanding of the array of problems and subjects we usually grapple with.

Alan Mulally's story illustrates this concept. He realized early in his managerial career that to become an effective leader, similar to Socrates, one should assist employees in uncovering their own skills and how they can contribute to the organization. This approach enables them to authentically express themselves and solve problems with greater creativity and effectiveness.

Alan Mulally could have easily become an authoritarian boss, much like Miranda Priestly, if his employee had simply obeyed. Thankfully, his employee was no Peter Gibbons, and instead of relinquishing control, he had the courage to speak up.

How can you actively employ the Socratic method more effectively in your daily personal and professional life?

The Socratic method can aid us in becoming more effective leaders, team members, and creative problem solvers. It encompasses six different categories of questions. Let's delve deeper into the various types of questions, accompanied by concrete examples:

- **Clarification:** "What do you mean by XYZ?" Great for understanding a problem.
- **Challenging assumptions:** "What is the underlying assumption of your hypothesis?" Great for coaching a struggling team member or addressing an aggressive email you may have received accusing you of something.
- **Evidence and reasoning:** "Can you provide supporting evidence to back up your argument?" When someone is presenting a new project and asking for funding.
- **Alternative viewpoints:** "What other points of view can you think of?" Useful in a coaching context.
- **Implications and consequences:** "What are the implications of

what you're saying?" When someone is making decisions that have significant consequences.

- **Challenging the question:** "What would have been a better question to ask?" When changing the way questions are posed becomes the norm, and you are helping teams ask better questions.

At its core, the premise that the Socratic method follows is that asking questions is a crucial first step in identifying a problem that should be solved or gaps in our knowledge that should be filled. As we just saw, the Socratic method framework uses different types of questions to either clarify particular problems, understand the underlying assumptions of an argument, seek more evidence, entertain various viewpoints, examine possible implications, or challenge the very question itself.

As with many other behaviors, activities, skills, and dispositions, asking meaningful questions is a practice that we gradually lose as we grow older. Some studies suggest that children ask around 40,000 questions between the ages of 2 and 5[4]. The number of questions dramatically decreases over time. The reason why children ask so many questions is that they are naturally curious and persistently strive to know whether the moon is made of cheese and whether Tom and Jerry are real.

Another, and more important reason why they ask so many questions, even if it can be extremely annoying at times, is that they never shy away from asking what's on their mind. If they don't understand something, they ask. If they want to figure out how something works, they ask. They don't self-censor as they would eventually do when

---

4   Harris, P. L. (2015). *Trusting What You're Told: How Children Learn from Others* (Reprint edition). Belknap Press.

they become self-conscious teenagers who don't want to be made fun of because they don't know how babies are made.

It seems as if there's an ever-present pressure to act as though we know what we're doing and talking about as we grow older. Not only is not knowing viewed as a bad thing but also inquiry somehow becomes frowned upon.

It's also fascinating how we are never really taught how to ask questions beyond the mere grammatical structure. Why do we even need to ask questions anyway? We already know what the problem is, and what we ought to do. We're experts! Or are we?

There are two primary contexts where we often need to ask questions: questions under uncertainty, where we aim to inquire to attain some sort of knowledge about ourselves, others, and the industry we work in (e.g., What are the emerging trends in our industry?), and questions to address a specific problem that we may be personally experiencing, which may involve others or problems in the workplace (e.g., Why did our sales decline in Q2?).

As such, in our role as inquirers, we can wear different hats and ask questions as:

- Curious explorers.
- Decision-makers.
- Impression managers.
- Empathetic listeners.
- Thought leaders.
- Problem solvers.
- Facilitators.

But how can we train ourselves to ask better, more engaging, and more meaningful questions? In other words, what does a good question look like versus a bad question?

A good question is often: open-ended, explorative, multifaceted, and disruptive. Of course, depending on the situation, the structure and content of questions may change, and what is normally considered a 'bad' question may, in fact, serve its purpose well. However, consider the following examples of good and bad questions:

Close-ended vs. Open-ended:

Instead of a close-ended question like, **"Did our last marketing campaign increase our sales?"** A better question would be an open-ended one urging us to broaden our perspectives and explore aspects that we may have initially overlooked. For example, a better question in this case could be, **"How did our last marketing campaign impact our sales, and what can we learn from it?"**

Assumptive vs. Explorative:

Instead of assuming a particular stance that could influence proposed solutions based on the wrong reasons, as in **"Why didn't our product perform well in the market?"** A better question would encourage us to explore different possible scenarios, for example, **"How has our product been received in the market, and what factors influenced its performance?"**

Narrow vs. Broad:

While narrow questions may sometimes be useful, broad questions often allow us to broaden our horizons and encourage us to explore more effective solutions and more innovative opportunities. For example, instead of asking "**How can we improve our product?**" A more interesting and broader question would be, "**What are the needs and expectations of our customers that aren't being met by our current product offerings?**"

Single-focused vs. Multi-faceted:

The same applies to single-focused vs. multi-faceted questions. Instead of limiting the explorative dimensions of our questions, for instance, by asking "**How can we reduce costs?**" We can adopt a more comprehensive perspective that examines different aspects of the issue at hand. In this case, a more meaningful question could be, "**How can we balance cost reduction while maintaining quality and customer satisfaction?**"

Conformity-driven vs. Disruptive :

And the most Socratic approach of them all. Instead of focusing on a more conformity-driven approach, such as, "**How can we do this the way it's always been done?**" We can adopt a more disruptive approach that would propel us to challenge our behavior and beliefs. For example, "**What if we approached this in a completely different way?**"

In addition to the Socratic framework, numerous other frameworks are available that focus on how to ask better questions. These include the 5 Whys, Bloom's Taxonomy, the STAR method, and other discovery methods applied in various contexts, such as interviewing, design thinking, law, medicine, detective work, and more. If you wish to explore this subject further, I recommend checking out the following books: "A More Beautiful Question" by Warren Berger and "Questions Are the Answer" by Hal Gregersen.

The primary aim of this section is to emphasize the importance of cultivating a questioning mindset and the significance of posing the right questions in the journey toward improved self-awareness, personal and professional development, and more effective problem-solving. As psychologist Carl Jung eloquently expressed, "To ask the right question is already half the solution to a problem."

Reflecting on these insights, it becomes evident that embracing self-awareness, challenging assumptions, and pursuing personal growth are indispensable components of fostering an authentic existence and effective leadership.

The path to achieving such a balanced and self-reflective mindset is often intricate and requires a catalyst to prompt us into action. This is where the essence of the trickster attitude comes into play.

Just as Socrates prompted us to question, the trickster encourages us to disrupt and explore unconventional avenues. It invites us to dance with uncertainty, challenge norms, and embark on uncharted paths.

By incorporating the trickster attitude into our journey of self-discovery, we can navigate the complexities of our own psyche and the world around us with an open mind and a spirit of creative exploration.

Chapter Three: Find and Embrace Your Inner Trickster

Nasreddin Hodja and His Donkey

Nasreddin Hodja, a renowned fictional character in Near Eastern folklore known for his wit and humor, walks through a bustling market alongside his son and their donkey. Various onlookers criticize them as they pass by.

The first group mocks them for not riding the donkey, prompting Hodja to oblige by asking his son to ride. The second group criticizes Hodja for allowing his son to ride instead of him, leading him to please them by riding the donkey himself. The third group criticizes them for not riding together, so they comply.

However, as the donkey becomes exhausted, a fourth group scorns them for overworking the animal. Exasperated, Hodja decides to carry the donkey and walk, eliciting laughter from onlookers and highlighting the absurdity of trying to please everyone.

This story humorously and cleverly illustrates the challenges of attempting to satisfy everyone, especially when the right context is missing. Hodja's decision to carry the donkey and walk presents a strange dilemma that encourages rethinking conventional norms and people's assumptions about suitable actions in particular situations, like how to make the best use of the donkey.

The story poses the question of how much one should prioritize pleasing others and conforming to societal norms versus staying authentic and pursuing activities in one's preferred manner, as long as no harm is caused to anyone.

Much like Socrates used questioning to provoke introspection, tricksters in myths and folklore employ a similar technique to challenge established norms and encourage reflection. Hodja, like Socrates, orchestrated a scenario that prompted the onlookers to introspect.

This was achieved not through forceful tactics or heated debates, but by engineering an absurd situation. This embodies the classic trickster attitude, urging us to approach situations and self-reflection with a sense of lightness. It encourages us to step back when we find ourselves deeply immersed in a customary way of doing things shaped by conventions, norms, and beliefs, and to reevaluate them without being overly serious about ourselves.

Hodja's reaction is a staple trickster attitude. Tricksters are commonly found in many mythical and folkloric narratives across all cultures. Some well-known tricksters include Loki from Norse mythology, Anansi from African folklore, Coyote from Native American mythology, Br'er Rabbit from African-American folktales, Hermes from Greek mythology, Nasreddin Hodja in Near Eastern folklore, and Sun Wukong, the Monkey King from Chinese mythology, among many others.

Tricksters as Disruptors of Systems

Tricksters play a significant role in myths and folklore tales, as they adopt a playful and humorous attitude that challenges established norms and conventions. Their actions serve to stimulate individuals within a given culture, encouraging them to raise probing questions and reflect upon their assumptions, beliefs, and societal norms. The enigmatic nature of the trickster figure adds to their intrigue, often leading them to be regarded as heroic figures in ancient mythologies.

Through their craftiness, magical abilities, and courage, tricksters disrupt unquestioned traditional systems, challenge specific practices and customs, and usher in new discussions on topics that would otherwise be considered taboo.

Psychologist Carl Jung believed that the trickster archetype represents a universal aspect of the human psyche. The trickster embodies qualities of chaos, unpredictability, and boundary-breaking, challenging established norms and societal conventions.

Jung saw tricksters as slackliners who navigate the fine line between our unconscious and conscious minds. This applies to both small and large scales, encompassing individuals, cultures, and societies.

What role do tricksters play? They enable us to confront our taboos, conventions, deepest desires, and true selves. The trickster stands beside us like a standup comedian, mirroring both our surface image and the deepest shadows of our unconscious. Its purpose isn't just to encourage self-embrace but also to serve as a launchpad for self-improvement.

Tricksters, with their clever antics and unconventional approaches, play a pivotal role in challenging societal norms. Just as Nasreddin Hodja's humorous actions prompt reflection, tricksters like Prometheus who stole fire from the gods to empower humans, or Anansi who cleverly outwitted larger foes, reveal that defying norms can lead to progress. Coyote's theft of fire from powerful beings in Native American myth similarly underlines how questioning hierarchies can benefit society. These trickster tales echo the potential of pushing boundaries and encourage leaders to rethink the status quo, sparking innovation and building resilience in the face of change.

The moral ambiguity and the cheerful, humorous attitude of tricksters in mythical narratives serve as reminders for societies to:

1. Keep themselves in check.
2. Continuously examine their assumptions.
3. Incorporate an element of uncertainty.
4. Not take themselves too seriously.
5. Recognize that system disruptors are catalysts for growth and innovation.

This is easier said than done. Developing a mindset that accounts for the trickster in us as individuals or as a group can be extremely difficult. Such stories don't usually end well either. Socrates, who was a true trickster, was sentenced to death because he was seen as a threat to the system. According to Jung, our ego plays an essential role in stopping us from resorting to the trickster in us when we most need it.

Keeping the Ego in Check

At the end of the day, it can be excruciating for both us and our egos to hear that we are not as good as we thought. Consider the example of Alan Mulally, mentioned earlier. What would you have done if you were in his place and an employee told you that you're not a good manager because you micromanage and expect your employees to become a carbon copy of you?

If you take yourself too seriously, you would likely shun such accusations and double down on your style of doing things, assuming your expertise. If you possess a trickster side, you would accept such criticism with levity, listen to feedback, and entertain new ideas to grow as a leader. But be cautious not to become an absolute conformist. Hodja, with his trickster demeanor, also imparts insights into the complexity of such situations.

Through a trickster-like approach, you can become more self-aware, delve into self-examination, and pinpoint your actual strengths and weaknesses to enhance your personal and professional life. This attitude enables you to reexamine assumptions, identify new pathways for innovation, and more.

Embracing a trickster-like stance lets you embrace vulnerability as a tool for growth, inspiring not only your own development but also that of those around you—an approach Socrates employed and one that Alan Mulally learned the hard way.

Let's revisit the character Peter Gibbons from "Office Space." How did he, once an absolute conformist who had relinquished all control, manage to reverse this situation?

Growing dissatisfied with his circumstances, he visits a hypnotist recommended by his girlfriend in a bid to liberate himself. The hypnosis takes a surprising turn when the hypnotist unexpectedly dies during the process.

As a result, Peter becomes trapped in a state almost similar to hypnosis, somewhat resembling the trickster attitude, straddling the boundary between consciousness and unconsciousness, and adopts a more relaxed demeanor. Over time, he begins to engage in activities aligned with his preferences, airing grievances, speaking his mind, pushing back against authority figures, and challenging established norms.

Through this process, Peter comes to realize that he is not leading an authentic life and that this disconnection is gradually isolating him. Employing his trickster-like approach, he identifies his areas of weakness and strength and acknowledges what he desires to cultivate, such as relationships with friends and his girlfriend. His journey serves as an illustration of how embracing a trickster-like mindset can disrupt conformist tendencies, nurturing innovation, self-awareness, and the audacity to occasionally liberate oneself from the confines of societal norms.

Ricardo Semler, A Trickster, A Maverick

Ricardo Semler frequently clashed with his father, Antonio Semler, over the direction SEMCO should pursue to stay afloat. As the head of the business, Antonio Semler vehemently opposed the diversification strategies Ricardo proposed. However, SEMCO, a Brazilian manufacturing company that originally specialized in shipbuilding, was, in fact, sinking.

In 1980, Antonio Semler finally decided to step down and passed the majority of the company's ownership to his son, Ricardo. At the age of 21, Ricardo had to step up and pull the struggling company forward. It was an uphill battle worse than that of Sisyphus. The first order of business as soon as he took office? Reduce the firm's top leadership by 60%.

Ricardo's experience at the helm of the company was an extremely fruitful learning curve. Under his leadership, SEMCO would eventually increase its annual revenue from $4 million in 1982 to approximately $200 million in 2003. He also grew the company from 90 employees to over 5,000. But it wasn't always roses and rainbows.

The ride was extremely bumpy. At the age of 25, Ricardo was diagnosed with an acute case of stress that threatened his health and his life. It was his first wake-up call, the catalyst for change, to reexamine his leadership style, his approach to management, and the importance of work-life balance.

Gradually over the years, Ricardo challenged the well-established traditional methods of management in favor of an unorthodox, decentralized, laid-back, employee-first approach. Through a trickster-like attitude, he started examining himself and questioning the assumptions that underpinned traditional management styles. By challenging the norm and established values, Ricardo was viewed with a certain sense of skepticism at first.

He adopted a more transparent tactic with his employees, removing complex hierarchical structures and relying on decentralized and smaller manufacturing units. He cut down unnecessary bureaucracy, shared the company's budget and balance sheets with employees, allowed them to work from anywhere they wanted, choose their working schedules, and determine their salaries and benefits. Unit managers and leaders were chosen by employees and were evaluated by them every six months. Employees were encouraged to pursue a work-life balance, seek innovation within the company, and explore their own interests outside the organization, without being constrained by rules and regulations. Instead, the company adopted a more organic approach that included a bottom-up standard of practice, which the employees helped develop.

In short, as Ricardo himself put it, he treated employees as adults capable of making decisions that contributed to the common good of the firm. He let them in on the decision-making process, ensured they were well-informed about the ins and outs of the financials, maintained open channels of communication, and encouraged employees to pursue meaningful work within the company and achieve a work-life balance.

Despite it being a manufacturing business that required a large number of employees to be present, the manufacturing units were able to determine the flow of work that best suited them to keep up with their key performance indicators while maintaining the well-being of the employees.

By adopting a trickster-like attitude, infused with a reflective and philosophical mindset, Ricardo Semler managed to challenge deeply-rooted beliefs about leadership and management styles, succeeding eventually in creating a productive, well-functioning, employee-friendly company underscored by a bottom-up, self-organizing dynamic.

Ricardo writes about his experiment in an interesting book called

"Maverick!: The Success Story Behind the World's Most Unusual Workplace." Over the years, Ricardo gradually reduced his involvement in the business and focused on other activities, like establishing a new educational methodology called LUMIAR that aims to transform the traditional educational model. It proposes a new way of approaching education, empowering students, and making their learning journey more meaningful and practical, echoing a Socratic-like approach.

But self-awareness, the Socratic method, and keeping our ego in check would be insufficient if we were not willing to shift our perspectives and see the problems we are facing from different angles.

In the following chapter, we will explore the importance of shifting our perspectives and examine the difference between the desire to win arguments vs. the need to solve problems.

Chapter Four: Shifting Perspectives

"Beware of the assumption that the way you work is the best way simply because it's the way you've done it before." — Rick Rubin

Embrace the Mess of Innovation, Problem Solving, and Change

In a talk titled "It's Time to Embrace the Mess,[5]" advertising executive and author Rory Sutherland reflects on the messiness and nonlinearity that frequently underlie the innovation process. While we might prefer to believe that innovation and problem-solving result from neat, linear, top-down processes driven by clean data gathering and analysis, the reality is more complex than that. Sutherland explains that the polished and structural approach to problem-solving and innovation, which the corporate world has adopted, is due to the proliferation of the "winning-argument" mindset.

Several reasons highlight why this is the case, as pointed out by Sutherland. First, the necessity to win an argument has become

---

[5]   https://youtu.be/TcRqBSSBYpc?si

crucial in the modern workplace. Before any decision can be made, it's necessary to obtain approval from various departments. Even before the creative process begins, an argument must be won.

Second, analytic thinking, or what Sutherland terms "reasoning forward," is easier to carry out than "reasoning backward", or synthetic thinking (explained below). Reasoning forward relies on constructing an argument in which the conclusion is derived from a presupposed set of premises, assumptions, beliefs, or existing data. It operates on the assumption that 'this is true, and therefore...'

Reasoning backward demands creativity because, instead of crafting an argument to prove a specific viewpoint, it delves into examining the existing problem and endeavors to solve it by asking the question: **What should be true or the case to find an effective solution to this problem?** This approach begins with a partially blank slate. Instead of working with existing assumptions or interpreting current data, you clear the way to metaphorically explore the field, discern the problem, and progressively work backward to solve it. As such, reasoning backward means starting with the desired solution and working backward step by step to determine the conditions that must be met to achieve that solution.

To illustrate the difference between forward and backward reasoning, consider the example Roger L. Martin provides in his book "A New Way to Think." He highlights the case of a consulting firm he once advised, whose clients were nonprofit organizations. One particular NGO was facing "starvation cycles" because more funds were donated to support direct costs, such as financing an educational program in Africa, rather than covering the initial development of such programs. Martin explains that the management of the NGO adopted forward reasoning because they assumed that since funding for indirect expenses was minimal, they needed to come up with rigorous arguments to convince the donors to allocate more money. However, following this process yielded no significant results. What Martin suggested was that they abandon their assumptions and listen to the donors first. After speaking with them, the organization found out that the donors were aware of the problem but were skeptical about the NGO's abilities to responsibly manage the funding for indirect costs. Once they figured out what needed to be the case to solve the problem, the NGO, alongside the donors, followed a reasoning backward approach to establish a solution to raise more funding for indirect expenses while maintaining the donors' trust.

Logical & Creative Reasoning

The distinction between analytic (logical) and synthetic (creative) reasoning is a central topic of discussion in philosophy. It is related to the various types of knowledge we can acquire, the tools we use to attain them, and the level of certainty we have about the truth of the knowledge that each mode of reasoning provides us.

Scottish philosopher David Hume (1711 — 1776), for instance, differentiates between analytic or demonstrative statements, and synthetic or probabilistic statements. According to Hume, analytic statements are those that are always necessarily true because they cannot be otherwise.

For example: linguistic and mathematical definitions, relations of ideas, and mathematical relations fall under such a category. When I assert that a bachelor is an unmarried man, this is true by definition and cannot be otherwise. Similarly, a triangle is, by definition, 3-sided;

otherwise, it would assume a different shape.

The truth value of these arguments doesn't rely on our experience, observation, or verification as they are true by definition, and the conclusion directly follows from the premises. Relations of ideas, Hume explains, do not furnish us with any novel knowledge about the world.

They only affirm that something is true based on preconceived assumptions, self-evident statements, and definitions. That's why analytical arguments about the existence of God make sense and might be true within the argument's scope[6]. Why? Because they operate within an analytic and demonstrative context where the conclusion's truth emanates from the definitions and assumptions. Do these arguments genuinely prove whether or not God exists in real life?

On the other side, synthetic statements require observation and experience to verify their accuracy. For example, a statement like

---

[6] For example, St. Anselm (1033 — 1109) presents in the "Proslogion" an argument for the existence of God based on the definition of the concept of God. The passage is quite complex, so I'm sharing the summarized form from the Internet Encyclopedia of Philosophy (Anselm: Ontological Argument for God's Existence).

"It is a conceptual truth (or, so to speak, true by definition) that God is a being than which none greater can be imagined (that is, the greatest possible being that can be imagined).

God exists as an idea in the mind.

A being that exists as an idea in the mind and in reality is, other things being equal, greater than a being that exists only as an idea in the mind.

Thus, if God exists only as an idea in the mind, then we can imagine something that is greater than God (that is, a greatest possible being that does exist).

But we cannot imagine something that is greater than God (for it is a contradiction to suppose that we can imagine a being greater than the greatest possible being that can be imagined.)

Therefore, God exists."

"a metal expands when heated" isn't demonstrative; it's a synthetic statement that melds concepts and ideas to communicate something new about how metals respond to heat.

The issue with these statements, as Hume informs us, is that they aren't demonstrative but rather probabilistic. In other words, while we can be almost certain that a piece of metal expands when heated, extending this certainty to an absolute statement such as "all metals expand when heated" becomes problematic. Why? Because the argument's nature and the statement are synthetic, not analytic.

Essentially, there's no inherent reason why it must unfailingly be true that metals expand when heated; we can never demonstrate this independently of experience. To verify the statement's truth, experimentation is necessary.

Here's a more intriguing twist: Since the truth of the statement relies on observation and experience, we can never assume that future results will mirror past experiences. It only takes one instance that contradicts the expected results for the generalized statement to be false.

This is what we refer to as the problem of induction. An often-cited example in this context is the discovery of black swans. People in Europe assumed that all swans were white until black swans were discovered in Western Australia by Dutch explorer Willem de Vlamingh and his crew.

Can Be Otherwise, Cannot Be Otherwise

In his book "A New Way To Think," Roger L. Martin highlights the importance of developing the skill to distinguish between things that cannot be changed due to necessity and things that can be altered through probabilistic approximation. This skill is crucial when addressing problems.

If you are attempting to construct a concrete building or an airplane, where stakes and risks are high, and you're dealing with laws of physics and established engineering norms, then analytic thinking is likely to be quite helpful. However, if the nature of the problem allows for alternative approaches, then it can be tackled from different perspectives, yielding multiple creative and potentially effective solutions.

Roger L. Martin and Rory Sutherland emphasize the significance of identifying the nature of the problems companies face. Is it a problem that cannot be altered? In that case, there's little room for debate, and analytic, forward, demonstrative reasoning and argumentation should take the lead.

But if it involves probabilistic, synthetic, backward reasoning, then collaborative, creative, and problem-solving approaches should prevail over winning an argument or debate.

When dealing with customers and human behavior or when solving a problem that doesn't strictly fall under the 'necessity' category, relying solely on data, winning arguments, and seeking evidence based on past experiences won't yield much help. Hence, reframing the approach from an assertive standpoint of "this is true, therefore" to an inquisitive perspective of "what ought to be true so that" is vital.

Why Winning an Argument Is Useless (More Often than Not)

Here are six reasons why winning an argument when addressing a problem that requires synthetic reasoning is futile:

1. You become more concerned about the soundness of the argument than the actual point you wish to convey.
2. You fall prey to a form of dogmatism, adopting a defensive stance regarding the purported argument.
3. As a consequence, you become confined by your arguments even before fully developing them.
4. It becomes perilous, as it leads to endless debates about arguments, *about arguments*, ultimately missing the point.
5. Attempting to pinpoint *the point* in an argument becomes fruitless, as others are more interested in refuting the argument than understanding it.
6. This results in an ego clash, where everyone strives to prove their intelligence, wit, and philosophical prowess over others.

In essence, winning arguments and proving a point restrict you to a narrow perspective. You perceive the world through a specific lens shaped by preexisting assumptions and beliefs. It can be rather difficult to break free from this and challenge yourself.

Solving the Insoles and Footwear Problem

To further illustrate this issue, consider a concrete example from my interview with Costas Papaikonomou, a product innovation veteran, entrepreneur, and impact investor. In his innovative consulting work, Costas approaches problem-solving with a mindset akin to Sherlock

Holmes. He emphasizes that if you want to solve problems, be creative, and innovate, you must actively seek out clues. The goal is to ask questions to gather these clues, rather than asking questions to find specific answers or, even worse, using leading questions that elicit yes or no responses.

Costas thinks that there's a hard line between the information-gathering phase and the solution-generation one. To illustrate this, Costas discussed how he and his team undertook a significant project to understand customer preferences and product performance for a big shoe polish and insoles brand.

Initially, the company followed a simplistic, top-down, approach: producing more of what sells well and reducing production of less popular items. This linear strategy didn't reflect the complex reality of customer preferences.

To gain deeper insights, Costas and his team traveled globally to study diverse markets. They discovered that customer behavior and needs varied significantly across different regions. For instance, in disposable-oriented cultures like North America, sneakers were popular and quickly discarded, while in places like Kenya, shoes were treated as valuable assets due to limited resources.

One aspect of their research focused on women's preferences in shoes. They realized through their clue-gathering research that comfort was approached differently by men and women. While men sought comfort, women were more concerned with pain management due to the discomfort caused by certain shoe designs. This led the team to develop innovative gel cushions tailored to alleviate pain in specific areas of the foot.

Costas emphasized that gathering clues and asking indirect questions was crucial for uncovering insights. Rather than receiving direct answers, they collected fragments of information that, when pieced together, formed a cohesive understanding of customer behavior.

He discussed the dichotomy between the questions asked and the answers obtained, emphasizing that these two aspects operate independently. He believed that extracting answers from the gathered clues required a collaborative effort and careful analysis. Costas underscored the significance of having a nuanced understanding of customer preferences and the value of asking the right questions to unlock meaningful insights.

This story highlights several important aspects that have been discussed so far about how nuanced and complex innovative, efficient, and creative problem-solving works. To begin with, taking a step back and questioning your assumptions is crucial. It's also vital to differentiate between what cannot be otherwise and what can be otherwise within the specific problem you're examining.

In the former, things must adhere to a particular set of rules and procedures to solve the problem, typically relying on analytic and forward reasoning. In the latter, it requires more than winning debates and analyzing data with preconceived notions, as solving a problem, in this case, demands backward, synthetic reasoning.

This is best achieved by suspending your beliefs, both literally and metaphorically, and actively seeking out clues, as Costas put it, rather than seeking immediate answers. Ideally, your questions should be open-ended and Socratic.

Costas sums it up nicely: When gathering clues to solve a problem, you should:

- "Assume you know nothing, or you'll miss all the interesting stuff. Be curious.
- Capture clues: anything that makes you wonder 'why?' Whether it's a consumer verbatim, a newspaper snippet, or a competing product.
- Be aware of your filters: make factual notes and observations only. Do not (yet) process the information — bring raw data."

In a way, winning arguments, and proving a point, is limiting you to a narrow perspective. You see the world through a particular lens, conditioned by assumptions and beliefs you already operate with. It can also be difficult to snap out of it and challenge yourself. How can you, in fact, overcome this predicament? Well, one step is to, as we already mentioned, become aware that this is a problem and to employ strategies like the Socratic framework to examine the assumptions and to seek growth.

Shifting Perspectives: A Plato Example

You also have to expose yourself to different viewpoints. One example to illustrate this comes from an interesting dialogue written by Plato called the Symposium.

In the "Symposium", Plato invites the readers to explore the concept and definition of 'love' from 7 different perspectives. The dialogue is structured in a way that does not offer us a clear definition of love but takes us on a journey of perspective shifting in order to understand the different layers and complexities of the concept, and how our experiences can influence our conceptions.

In this dialogue, a group of notable people attending a banquet take turns to give speeches about love. Each one of them ends up giving an account of it that reflects their profession.

For example, the lawyer's speech focuses on love from a legal perspective, the physician from a biological and physical perspective, the comedian provides a comic account, and the tragedian a tragic account. Towards the end of the dialogue, Socrates provides a synthesis of the different viewpoints and ends up offering a philosophical account of the concept.

The importance of this dialogue is that it invites the reader to explore a concept from different perspectives without the need to take sides. It is a dialogue that allows us to explore and discover new ideas in a constructive manner. Entertaining alternative perspectives does not mean that we should agree with the viewpoints shared by others. However, the goal of exercises such as the one presented above is to foster an understanding of alternative viewpoints, build up better communication and negotiation channels, and establish some sort of common ground to facilitate problem-solving.

Plato's "Symposium" is a brilliant illustration of a 'Mastermind' gathering. Instead of becoming emotionally entangled in the definition of love, each presenter shared their unique perspective while fostering an open-minded and inquisitive attitude toward the other speakers. They also attentively listened to their presentations.

Such exchanges broaden the participants' perspectives, enabling them to challenge biases, avoid oversimplifying complex topics, address their blind spots, and encourage a collaborative mindset that motivates them to address problems with greater creativity while accounting for the multifaceted nature of the topic at hand.

Return to Office: A Case Study

Now let's take this a step further and explore an emerging problem as a case study for which we haven't had any clear solution yet.

Should you go back to the office or not? This is one of the countless heated debates that companies, CEOs, VCs, and people on social media are engaging in.

One faction advocates the stance that employees should return to the office. The other argues that employees should have the choice to either work remotely or go back to the office.

Both sides provide reasons to support their stance. Let's delve deeper into this matter. The clash centers around conclusions.

One side reaches the conclusion that returning to the office is preferable. The other side reaches the opposite conclusion.

If you aim to win the argument, solving the problem becomes challenging. Why? This is because both perspectives hold merit. Why? The arguments presented are built upon a series of assumptions or premises that lead to these conclusions.

These assumptions can be either correct or incorrect. Yet, while striving to demonstrate the truth and logical coherence of your argument, the focus often shifts to disproving the other side instead of engaging in a dialogue to resolve the issue.

What are some of these assumptions?

For remote work: flexibility enhances productivity, reduces commuting stress, cuts costs, and promotes work-life balance.

For returning to the office: concerns about security, accountability, collapsing work-life boundaries, endangering company culture, and a lack of collaboration.

What is the problem being addressed here? Let's formulate it in the form of a question:

How can organizations and employees effectively balance the desire for flexible remote work arrangements with the need for productive collaboration, employee well-being, company culture, and operational efficiency in an evolving work landscape? Too wordy. Let's simplify it:

How can we strike the right balance between remote work and office-based collaboration to ensure productivity, employee well-being, and a robust company culture? Do we want to win a debate or solve a problem?

If our goal is problem-solving, then more effort must be invested in introspection, questioning our assumptions, and building an empathetic stance by actively listening to understand opposing views.

Do I possess the answer? No. **However, by clarifying the problem and comprehending the underlying assumptions presented by each viewpoint, we can establish an environment that facilitates**

more effective idea exchange.

One reason why this debate is intriguing is because it highlights the need for control. Employees seek control over choices, work environment, and arrangements, while employers aim to maintain control over organizational processes, employee monitoring, etc.

Change has disrupted the perspectives of both sides. Yet, a debate that prioritizes winning over problem-solving leads nowhere. A philosophical mindset can aid in addressing these issues, offering a fresh perspective.

Traditional problem-solving often revolves around a competition of ideas, where winning arguments emerge as the ultimate goal. True problem-solving demands an alternative approach, grounded in empathy, self-awareness, and a genuine desire to understand the assumptions of others. By cultivating a mindset of curiosity and open-mindedness, individuals can transcend the ego-driven pursuit of being right, creating a harmonious space for meaningful dialogue and collaborative problem-solving.

The return-to-office debate presents itself as a compelling case to explore the points discussed so far, particularly due to its unsolved nature and the requirement for innovative solutions.

The first question we need to ask ourselves is as follows: Does our decision-making rely on analytic or synthetic reasoning in this case? Could parts of this problem be different or not? To begin with, we are not dealing with a straightforward issue here.

Clearly, if the nature of work demands employees to be physically present, then there's no debate there. However, if the nature of the work doesn't necessitate the constant physical presence of employees, then the question arises: How do we approach this problem? By engaging in debates and presenting arguments based on preconceived notions, assumptions, and available data? Or by venturing out and asking ourselves what needs to be true in order to collaboratively address this problem, leading to creative and innovative solutions?

If the answer is the latter, then it's crucial to conduct market research with a Socratic or Sherlock Holmes hat on to search for clues. What do employers and employees really want (This sounds like a good movie title, one I would definitely watch, what about you?)? How can we devise a solution that benefits both parties and ensures everyone's contentment? What underlies the assumptions, and how can we adjust our perspectives, cultivate empathy, and listen more attentively to comprehend the standpoint of those involved?

I have been oscillating between introspection and interpersonal relationships involving collaboration and teamwork. This is because one of the fundamental skills for solving problems more effectively and collaboratively requires a deep sense of awareness.

On a personal level, this can mean self-awareness, as we've previously discussed, encompassing an understanding of our strengths, limitations, desires, emotions, goals, and an awareness of our physical surroundings, be it at home, the office, or the gym. On a professional level, things become a bit more complex. The reality is that it is not easy to have everyone on the same page, and it's likely that different individuals within a company or team will have varying degrees of self-awareness.

Some employees, managers, and executives might be dogmatic and cling to their worldviews, just like Miranda Priestly, making decisions that align with their convictions without much inquiry or self-doubt. Others might demonstrate more awareness.

Concluding remarks: Philosophical Quest

But before even thinking about how to create an environment that fosters self-awareness, questions assumptions, and nurtures a philosophical mindset, it's essential to emphasize the importance of this approach.

Much like cultivating a philosophical mindset at an individual level serves as a catalyst for personal growth, teams and companies can also benefit from such a mindset. It allows them to recognize opportunities for development, incorporate fresh perspectives, and collaborate collectively to creatively and effectively resolve problems, shifting the focus from winning arguments to problem-solving.

The crux of all this is to grasp that a philosophical mindset isn't a final destination achievable through specific tricks, hacks, or shortcuts. It's a continuous journey, a quest, demanding periodic self-assessment, reflection, asking meaningful questions, and establishing a conversational space to explore diverse viewpoints, shift perspectives, and acknowledge that much of our unwavering beliefs and dogmatism arise from an excessive desire to control and make sense of our surroundings. The antidote would be to solicit and absorb feedback, embrace a trickster attitude, and gain insights from oneself, others, and the world around us.

In the end, the pursuit of innovative, efficient, and creative problem-solving requires a blend of analytic and synthetic reasoning, a philosophical perspective, and a resilient spirit. By embracing these principles, we can navigate the ever-evolving landscape of challenges with curiosity, empathy, and the determination to uncover solutions that transcend the boundaries of winning debates.

Navigating uncertainty and adversity, as well as combating stress, anxiety, and fear that we experience in our personal and professional lives, pose some serious challenges. In the next part, we will address some practical ways to deal with uncertainty and adversity more effectively by examining the Stoic framework. We will also explore how to combat boredom and the ensuing anxiety and stress by searching for meaning in life and work following the suggestions of existentialist philosophers, including the Austrian psychiatrist and philosopher Viktor Frankl and the French philosopher Jean-Paul Sartre.

II

Uncertainty, Adversity, and the Quest for Meaning

"There are things up to us and things not up to us. Things up to us are our opinions, desires, aversions, and, in short, whatever is our own doing. Things not up to us are our bodies, possessions, reputations, offices, or, in short, whatever is not our own doing." — Epictetus

Part Two: Introduction

The other day, as I strolled through my home city of Salamanca, I observed and pondered the following while crossing several streets: some pedestrian signals had countdown timers, but others did not. I wondered whether the timer would make the wait more bearable, and, if so, what exactly about this arrangement made it so.

I obviously did not make any new discoveries here, but it was one of those realizations that strikes you like lightning when you start making all sorts of random associations relevant to a particular subject you're contemplating. In this case, I was thinking about uncertainty and the ensuing stress and anxiety we experience because of it.

My initial hunch was that even if the wait to cross the street was the same, it felt like forever on the one without the countdown timer. Due to this uncertainty about when it would turn green, waiting would become even more annoying, especially if you are in a hurry.

In contrast, when you're certain about the duration of the wait, the element of uncertainty is eliminated, and you have enough information to incorporate into your decision-making process to account for it. In short, waiting would be significantly less stressful, particularly if you're in a hurry.

This observation led me to delve into how we respond to and manage uncertainty. During my research, I came across a study[7] published in Nature titled "Computations of uncertainty mediate acute stress responses in humans." The research team found that the pain experienced when one is certain about receiving a shock is less than the pain felt when one is uncertain about it.

Knowing the exact arrival time of the train, bus, or taxi makes the wait more bearable, and the greater the certainty, the better. For example, when you can track the taxi's location through GPS, not only does the waiting time become easier to endure, but I would venture to say it even becomes more entertaining.

You can check your app every now and then to make sure the driver is heading straight to where you are and did not decide to take a detour to stop by the bookshop to buy a Hegel book — who would do that anyway? But you get the gist.

We crave certainty, even though on some occasions we seek the thrill of surprise when the outcome is pleasant, particularly when reading a suspenseful novel or watching an action movie. Even then, we would still prefer to be certain that the hero will survive.

In cases of adversity, such as receiving an electric shock, as per the study cited above we handle the event much better if we are certain it will happen. Perhaps this is because we train and mentally prepare ourselves to confront such adversity, especially when it is inevitable.

You want to be certain about the estimated project deadline you

---

[7] https://www.nature.com/articles/ncomms10996

requested from the team, certain about meeting the budget, certain about receiving a raise, certain about the product's success, certain about the plane departing on time, and so on.

And because we crave certainty, we incorporate it into our system as creatures of habit, as Scottish philosopher David Hume asserts.

We eat our food every day, acting as if it will certainly nourish us, even though there's a slight chance it may be poisoned. We act as though we are certain that the car is right where we parked it, even though there's a slight chance it might not be. We act as if the sun will "rise" tomorrow, even though there's an extremely negligible probability that it might not. We make business and personal decisions about the future, assuming that things will go as planned: asking someone out, reaching out to a potential client, launching a new product, starting a new business, buying a house, and so forth.

But the reality is that life is quite unpredictable, and it doesn't always align with our expectations. Deep down, we know this, even though we often act as if we are certain about the future.

However, the disconnect between our expectations and reality, coupled with the inherent uncertainty of nature and life, triggers a range of emotions in us as human beings, including anxiety, stress, frustration, and despair.

To combat these emotional challenges, we often create various plans and spread our investments to reduce the impact of uncertainty. Handling financial, career, and other tangible uncertainties can be quite manageable. However, addressing the psychological and existential aspects of dealing with daily uncertainty, along with our natural tendency to avoid unknown risks and dangers, can be more difficult.

Stress, anxiety, despair, and a full spectrum of emotions can be difficult to cope with, particularly because these experiences are subjective and often challenging to articulate. Each individual's reality is unique.

For instance, you might be greatly distressed if your flight is canceled but have no issues losing a million dollars, depending on your situation and context. You may have navigated the global lockdown during the COVID pandemic better than others but still struggle to manage your feelings and reactions when dealing with a difficult client or employee.

In recognizing the complexity of human emotions and how these subjective experiences can shape and influence our responses to adversity and suffering, philosophers have attempted to provide practical frameworks to equip us with the necessary tools for preparing and navigating through turbulent times.

Some philosophers, schools of thought, and philosophical movements even discuss how uncertainty and randomness can lead to a sense of existential anxiety, suggesting that we should seek meaning in the face of uncertainty and adversity to better navigate challenging periods.

In the following chapters, we will explore the Stoic framework for navigating uncertainty and adversity in Chapter 5, and in Chapter 6, we will examine some of the tips and remedies offered by psychiatrist Viktor Frankl and other philosophers within the existentialist tradition to overcome suffering and anxiety.

Chapter 5: Navigating Uncertainty & Adversity

"All honorable means of protecting ourselves from harm are not only permitted but commendable. The chief function of constancy is to patiently endure those hardships that cannot be avoided." — Montaigne

Zeno's Shipwreck

When Zeno set sail from Cyprus to Athens with a ship full of purple dye, his primary business supply, he was certain that he would safely reach his destination, conduct successful commercial transactions, generate profits, and return home safely to prepare for another venture. To his dismay, the day did not unfold as expected. He experienced a shipwreck shortly before reaching Athens.

While he remained physically unharmed, the accident took a psychological toll on him, and he also lost his entire business, leaving him with nothing. Despite the unpleasantness of the situation, Zeno endeavored to comprehend the abrupt turn of events as he found himself ashore. "What now?" he pondered.

A whirlwind of emotions, including anger, frustration, stress, anxiety, and various inexplicable feelings, overwhelmed him. What had caused this misfortune? Was it his own doing? What course of action should he now pursue? Before I proceed, here's a joke I wrote.

When Zeno of Citium found himself shipwrecked due to a fierce storm, he fortunately survived the ordeal, though he did lose his entire business in the process. In an attempt to recover his losses, he headed straight to the insurance office to file a claim. However, unfortunately, the assessment was unfavorable, as they attributed it to an "act of the divine," leaving Zeno without compensation. In a fit of anger and frustration, he stormed out to the Stoa and founded an entire school of philosophy called Stoicism, aiming to encourage people to read their insurance policies before signing them.

Insurance policies aside, Zeno had a lot of work to do on emotional and existential levels. In Athens, he embarked on a soul-searching journey in hopes of finding a guide on how to manage the myriad sentiments that gripped him and how to be better prepared for similar incidents in the future. Zeno was trying to make sense of what had just happened.

He started hanging out with different philosophy communities. Athens, the epicenter of intellectual activity back then, was home to various philosophical schools, each boasting their own doctrines and perspectives.

These groups subscribed to particular worldviews, influencing how they understood the universe and their ideas on better governance, politics, economics, and citizenship.

Zeno was not all that amused, though. All the groups he came in contact with were addressing legitimate issues such as becoming better citizens, living a good life, and proposing theories about the nature of reality, but none were concerned with the problem he had gone through.

His questions were simple, but the answers were not as straightforward: How should we account for, prepare for, and handle events characterized by uncertainty? How does uncertainty impact our decision-making process? How can we effectively manage the range of emotions—fear, anxiety, stress, anger, frustration, and fury—that overwhelm us before, during, and after experiencing adversity and uncertainty? Is uncertainty inherent in the world, and if so, how can we harness it to our advantage?

Uncertainty, adversity, risk, and the potential for financial, commercial, and personal loss were not topics directly addressed by the groups Zeno came into contact with. He continued to survey the market, learn about existing accounts, synthesize information, and engage in introspection. He used his knowledge and experience to create and develop a new school of thought, primarily centered on managing risk, uncertainty, and adversity.

This school of thought would later be recognized as Stoicism, named after the location where Zeno and his students gathered: the Stoa, a covered walkway or colonnade adjacent to the marketplace in Athens.

I won't delve deeply into the history of Stoicism beyond the mere anecdotes, but it's intriguing how this school of thought, founded around 300 BCE, is immensely popular today, particularly within the business and startup spheres, as well as among executives and CEOs.

This popularity could be attributed either to the highly practical tips Stoicism offers that resonate with the business and entrepreneurial mindset (after all, Zeno himself was a merchant), or it may be due to the effective marketing efforts of proponents of Stoicism over the past 30 years. However, the precise reason is not of paramount importance, is it?

Numerous books take a closer look into Stoicism or promote Stoic approaches for coping with challenges and uncertainty. Some notable works include William Irvine's "A Guide to the Good Life: The Ancient Art of Stoic Joy," Ryan Holiday's "The Obstacle Is the Way," and Ward Farnsworth's "The Practicing Stoic." These books offer valuable insights into Stoicism and how to adopt a Stoic perspective. For a thorough exploration of Stoicism, I recommend reading these books, as I won't cover it extensively here.

Instead, the focus of this chapter is to highlight a few aspects and frameworks of Stoicism that I believe could be beneficial for business leaders and professionals in light of the topics I previously discussed, particularly in the context of questioning our assumptions and posing meaningful questions.

In the previous chapters, I touched upon the theory of control expounded by Will Storr in his book "The Science of Storytelling." This theory explains that, for various evolutionary and other reasons, we are inherently wired, inclined, and predisposed to control the world around us because it provides a sense of security and helps us make sense of our reality and environment.

We often achieve this by trusting our senses, forming beliefs and opinions about what works and what doesn't, what is safe and isn't, establishing societal norms to maintain order, and frequently categorizing and naming things.

Our desire and necessity for control are deeply ingrained in how we interact with the world, others, and ourselves. We yearn to maintain a sense of control, and in extreme cases, this desire can manifest in various unpleasant ways in our personal and professional lives, such as paranoia, distrust, and micromanagement.

In ordinary circumstances, it is comforting to have everything under control: our personal life, business decisions, endeavors, team members, project management, development, customer and employee satisfaction, and where we see ourselves in five years.

We come across as responsible people, who care for our future, and are ambitious, knowledgeable, wise, trustworthy, and hardworking when we exude a confident attitude in our ability to keep things under control. People respect that.

Consequently, we tend to pursue and cultivate this desire further, until, one day, as in the case of Zeno, we experience a proverbial shipwreck, causing the illusion of control to sink.

Recently, I came across a social media post about how, in order to thrive in the business world, one ought to reject the passivity and lackluster attitude of Stoicism and instead embrace an assertive, ambitious, and gritty mindset. The post asserted that one should be in control to achieve great things. It also emphasized the importance of having strong convictions that serve as a driving force for improvement, growth, and advancement.

I found this post interesting because it depicted Stoicism as a school of thought advocating passivity and a lack of ambition, and it underscored the importance of being in control and having a drive to achieve great things.

Zeno may have held a similar viewpoint until a few moments before he lost all his business. This external, unfortunate event acted as a catalyst for introspection and change for him. Subsequently, he ventured into the unknown to examine his belief system and convictions in an attempt to learn from his experience and take the necessary precautions and preemptive measures to avoid a similar outcome in the future.

Control, Emotions, and Luck in Stoicism

But is this really what Stoicism advocated? A passive, indifferent mentality towards things because what's the point anyway? Not really. Things are a bit more nuanced than that.

If there's one takeaway from Stoicism, **it's that there are things we can control and things we cannot control — I will reiterate this point frequently in the upcoming paragraphs.** So, we would be better off directing our efforts toward what we can control and thinking of more effective ways to either manage, prevent, or leverage what we cannot control to our advantage.

Here's an example from "Friends" to briefly illustrate the point. In Season 5, Episode 9, titled "The One with Ross's Sandwich," Ross is going through a rough time with his impending second divorce and eviction. He's visibly stressed and feels that things are falling apart in his life. Metaphorically speaking, the only thing that had been keeping his life and sanity together was a leftover turkey sandwich his sister Monica prepared for him. What makes this sandwich special, he explains, is the extra gravy-soaked slice of bread Monica adds in the middle, which Ross affectionately calls the "moistmaker."

Early in the episode, Ross angrily explains to his friends at the Central Perk coffee shop that someone at work had eaten his sandwich, ignoring the clear note that stated it was his.

Later in the episode, Ross experiences a nervous breakdown when his boss confesses to eating the sandwich but assures Ross that there might still be some leftover pieces in the trash because "it was too big to finish." This proves to be the straw that broke the camel's back for Ross.

What can we learn from this story? First, if it's not food you brought with you to work, it's better to avoid eating it if you don't want to end up in a fight with someone.

At face value, it might seem like a trivial example. You might be thinking to yourself, as Chandler from the group points out, that it's just a sandwich, and that there's no need to go berserk over the fact that someone accidentally, and without your permission, ate it. It's just a sandwich, no big deal! Or maybe not.

This incident, like many others in life and business, illustrates a crucial distinction that Zeno and the Stoics would explore and reflect on. Namely, there are things within our control and things beyond our control. Recognizing this fact is the first step in understanding how we can reduce the impact of events outside our control and manage our emotions accordingly.

Ross took all the necessary precautions to ensure that no one ate his sandwich, even leaving a note. Despite that, his boss, who was being inconsiderate for doing so, went ahead and consumed it.

Similarly, while more serious, Zeno recognized that there was little he could do to prevent the shipwreck. He had taken all the essential preparations, but due to reasons beyond his direct control, presumably adverse weather conditions, the ship sank.

Did the accident hinge on his decision-making process? Given the limited technology of the time for tracking weather conditions, Zeno had little leeway to anticipate a storm. His control extended to ensuring the ship's seaworthiness and the captain's skill in navigating turbulent waters.

In her book "Thinking in Bets," Annie Duke explains that under uncertainty, the outcomes of our decisions often do not accurately reflect their quality. In real life, much like in poker, our decisions are just one part of the equation, with luck playing a significant role.

Luck, in this case, is another way of accounting for all the events and outcomes that don't really depend on us or how great our decision-making, preparation, and training are.

The Stoics believed that certain aspects of decision-making and management are within our control, and influenced by our preparation and judgment. However, they recognized that other factors, such as external events and the actions of others, are beyond our control. These external factors, often referred to as luck by Annie Duke, can be either favorable or unfavorable, resulting in either good or bad luck.

It might not seem like a monumental realization at first, but upon closer consideration, you might notice a significant disconnect between our expectations and reality due to our inherent desire for control.

Frustrations arise when things don't go as expected or planned, leading to easily triggered reactions such as anger, disappointment, anxiety, and stress.

Such events that disrupt our plans can range from Ross's sandwich to Zeno's shipwreck. You may have had your flight canceled, causing you to miss a connecting flight and an important job interview. You may not have been able to secure your dream job or motivate your team to work on a project with the same enthusiasm as you. You may not have been able to elicit laughs from the public at the comedy store. You may have lost your job during the COVID pandemic or during mass tech layoffs. You may have lost your business or savings due to adverse economic conditions, recession, high inflation, and more.

But on the other side of the coin, you may have had all the necessary prerequisites and experience to get the job, worked diligently on your comedy gig, prepared thoroughly for your job interview, or put your heart and soul into the job you lost. Yet, things still didn't unfold as expected. Luck, uncertainty, and adversity, the Stoics understood, may disrupt all our plans.

So, the key question to consider regarding Zeno and Ross is: How should they have reacted in such circumstances?

The Stoics would approach the challenge of uncertainty and adversity from two distinct perspectives. One centers on managing emotions and preparing for and responding to adverse circumstances.

The other centers on the decision-making process, aiming to either mitigate, manage, or leverage uncertainty and adversity to our advantage.

In the following discussion, we will explore some of the Stoic frameworks and principles for navigating uncertainty and adversity while considering these two aspects.

"Good character, good intention, and good actions." — Marcus Aurelius

You may be thinking reality is more complex than just things we can control and things we cannot. You are absolutely right. Things aren't binary or that simplistic. However, simplifying our understanding can often be a useful starting point before diving into the subtleties. Within the Stoic philosophy, we encounter a three-fold categorization that helps us navigate this complexity:

1. **The Uncontrollable:** This category encompasses external events (like the weather), other people's opinions, thoughts, behavior, decisions, reactions, as well as the unchangeable aspects of the past and the uncertain nature of the future. In Stoicism, these are considered beyond our direct control.
2. **The Controllable:** Within this realm, we find our thoughts, values, judgments, beliefs, opinions, decisions, and the actions we choose to undertake. Stoicism emphasizes that these are areas where we possess agency and influence, and thus where our focus should be directed.
3. **The Partially Controllable:** Stoicism also acknowledges the existence of a third category, which includes our instincts, immediate visceral reactions, and desires. While we may not have

complete mastery over these aspects, Stoicism encourages us to exert some influence through self-awareness and discipline.

In essence, this Stoic framework allows us to embrace the multifaceted nature of our interactions with the world. It reminds us that control isn't a simplistic binary but rather a spectrum of influence and agency. This understanding can guide us in directing our efforts toward what truly matters in the face of life's challenges.

I want to focus first on what is partially controllable and address some misconceptions about Stoicism.

The term "stoic" has acquired a somewhat peculiar definition in modern dictionaries. Nowadays, it is used to describe someone who withstands hardships without complaint, remains emotionally indifferent, and maintains a poker face in the face of adversity.

While a poker face can help in bluffing and may improve one's luck in poker, it contradicts the Stoic approach to emotional management.

The Stoics did not aim to suppress or eradicate sentiments; instead, their focus was on how to acknowledge and effectively manage them. This is where the partially controllable category comes into play.

As humans, we are governed not only by our rational faculty but also by a mosaic of emotions, desires, instincts, affections, and more that compose our identity. Suppressing these sentiments would mean eliminating a significant part of what makes us human.

If you were to experience a shipwreck like Zeno, you would, of course, be vexed and frustrated. If someone ate your sandwich, just like in the case of Ross, you might be livid and feel the urge to punch someone in the face. Similarly, if someone wronged you, mistreated you, or insulted you or someone you know.

If your colleague is being inconsiderate, you may naturally feel like snapping at them. If someone cuts in line, you might automatically feel furious. If someone cracked a joke at your expense or at the expense of someone you like, just like in Will Smith's case, your initial reaction may be to slap them—poor Chris Rock.

The same applies to desires, affections, and so on. But the point is not to suppress these emotions and become zombie-like. The goal is to understand where these emotions are coming from and learn how to manage them, channeling them in a way that avoids causing harm or backfiring in the long run.

The most essential first step in managing our emotions more effectively is to understand how we process things and occurrences. According to the Stoics, there exists an additional stage that takes place between an event and our reaction to it. During this phase, we often swiftly categorize the event as either positive or negative, and our response follows suit. This is what the Stoics call judgment.

Judgment

> "Remember that what is insulting is not the person who abuses you or hits you, but the judgment about them that they are insulting... another person will not do you harm unless you wish it; you will be harmed at just that time at which you take yourself to be harmed." — Epictetus

Imagine you're touring a foreign city where you don't speak the language. You enter a store and attempt to communicate with the owner, but the language barrier makes it challenging. Despite your best efforts, effective communication seems impossible. After a few minutes of hand gestures and efforts to bridge the linguistic gap, you express gratitude and prepare to leave the store, empty-handed.

As you step outside, the store owner murmurs something with a smile on their face. Your initial impression is positive – you believe you had a pleasant interaction with a friendly shop owner.

However, another customer who witnessed the exchange approaches you with a concerned expression. They explain that the store owner had actually uttered an insult, not a kind remark.

Assuming, for the sake of this story, that this person is telling the truth, you stand there, momentarily perplexed and taken aback. Your perception of the situation had been entirely different.

Consider how your reaction might have shifted. The event itself remains unchanged, but your response has transformed. Initially, you interpreted the owner's actions as friendly; however, upon learning the words' true meaning, your reaction altered.

It's true that the person uttered foul words with the aim of insulting you. But this raises a crucial question: Is the feeling of being insulted solely determined by the intentions of the person delivering it, or does our perception and judgment play a significant role? How does our interpretation of events affect our emotional responses?

In this case, it becomes evident that feeling insulted lies within the observer's mind. First, they interpret the message, then assign a value to it – in other words, they determine whether the message is good or bad – and finally, they react accordingly.

This process of interpretation and value-assignment is what the Stoics referred to as judgment. According to the Stoics, external events, actions, and messages are value-neutral; they possess neither inherent positivity nor negativity. It is we who interpret and assign value to them.

Let me clarify one point before we move forward. You might wonder, "How can an action be considered value-neutral when someone is clearly attempting to harm me, maybe physically?" This is a valid concern. The Stoics would indeed see such actions as wrong or a vice. However, even though an action is deemed wrong because it could cause harm, the Stoics would not assign a value of good or bad to it based on the fact that it's happening to them.

Instead, they would approach it differently. To illustrate this concept quickly, my friend Rudi shared an idea from the Buddhist tradition called the "empty boat." Imagine you've just finished painting your boat and are on a foggy lake. Suddenly, another boat crashes into yours, and you become furious, shouting at the person steering the boat. But upon closer inspection, you realize that the boat is empty. In that moment, your anger and frustration subside.

Likewise, the Stoics would view actions directed at us as empty boats. They do this because they understand that we cannot fully control other people's actions. What we can control is our own response, ensuring it's not impulsive and doesn't worsen the situation. By treating the situation as though an empty boat has collided with us, we can maintain composure, which positions us better to seek justice or, in extreme cases, to defend ourselves, protect ourselves, or stand up for ourselves in the most rational, composed, and effective way we have at our disposal.

While you may disagree with this view, I encourage you to momentarily set aside your perspective and adopt the Stoic viewpoint. The Stoics believe that we determine whether an event is good or bad based on our interpretation, and our judgment of something being good or bad influences our behavior.

To simplify this, let's begin with two examples: desires and aversions. In life, there are things we desire and actively pursue, such as landing a dream job. Conversely, there are things we aim to avoid, like losing our life savings. These desires and aversions are inherent to our nature.

The Stoics aim to remove an additional layer of complexity: the judgment of these desires and aversions as inherently good or bad. Why? Because this added layer introduces unnecessary stress and anxiety into how we approach life.

For example, if you view getting your dream job as inherently good, failing to secure the position intensifies your disappointment. Similarly, if you perceive losing your savings as inherently bad, the actual loss becomes more distressing.

This complexity, the Stoics argue, traps us within labels and judgments.

> "Everything depends on opinion. Ambition, luxury, greed, all look back to opinion; it is according to opinion that we suffer. Each man is as wretched as he has convinced himself

he is." — Seneca, Epistles

By refraining from categorizing events as intrinsically good or bad, or by recognizing that you are engaging in this act of judgment, you can navigate adversity and uncertainty more smoothly. Rather than getting entangled in reminiscing over challenges, you approach these situations with preparedness, becoming adept at making reasoned decisions without unnecessary pressure.

According to the Stoics, this equates to having an opinion because it is rooted in our interpretation, and shaped by our beliefs. In simpler terms, understanding that our opinions are influenced by how our minds judge things as good or bad empowers us to control our reactions before, during, and after positive or negative experiences. This enables us to avoid impulsive actions.

The Stoics assert that impulsiveness isn't an immediate and automatic reaction; it is a response based on judgment — the determination of whether a situation is good or bad. So, the next time someone makes a joke at your or someone else's expense, consider where the impulse to react comes from. Is it because you perceive the joke as insulting and bad?

If so, that's your interpretation. If you pause and consider an alternative perspective, you may find a more effective response.

Stoicism's primary objective is to illuminate the complexity of our minds. Understanding this complexity helps us to navigate uncertainty and adversity effectively by focusing on what we control: our actions, reactions, judgments, virtues, and character.

"If any external thing causes you distress, it is not the thing itself that troubles you, but your own judgment about it. And this you have the power to eliminate now." — Marcus Aurelius, Meditations

Returning to our insult analogy, the Stoics extend this concept to various facets of life, illustrating their fundamental belief that events themselves are neither intrinsically good nor bad. It is our judgments and interpretations that ascribe them with value. Consider this perspective in the context of modern life:

Natural Elements: Think about adverse weather conditions – storms, heat waves, or cold snaps. These are natural occurrences, devoid of inherent goodness or badness. Their impact on us is shaped by how we perceive and respond to them.

Workplace Dynamics: In the modern workplace, scenarios like job rejection, termination, or promotions are common occurrences. These events, too, lack inherent moral value; they derive it from our perspectives.

Life's Inevitabilities: Aging is an undeniable part of the human experience. While growing older may not be enjoyable, it remains a natural facet of life. The judgment of whether it is good or bad is subjective.

Challenging Social Situations: Facing insults or ill-treatment is undoubtedly challenging. However, these circumstances are also neutral; their significance hinges on our interpretation and response.

Unforeseen Disruptions: Adverse weather conditions can disrupt plans, but they carry no intrinsic negativity. We can't control these external events, but we can control our reactions to them.

Financial Ups and Downs: Financial losses or business setbacks, as well as wealth accumulation, are devoid of inherent moral value. It is our judgments and attachments that confer positive or negative connotations.

The Stoics recognized the innate human drive for ambition – the pursuit of success, skill enhancement, personal enjoyment, wealth, social relationships, and contributions to society. However, they cautioned against fixating excessively on these goals.

The Stoic approach advises us to avoid categorizing situations as intrinsically good or bad as they occur. Instead, we should acknowledge the presence of adversity, uncertainty, and our desires or aversions, maintaining a balanced perspective.

In practical terms, the Stoics emphasize that events themselves do not possess inherent moral worth; rather, it is our responses that determine whether our actions align with virtue, the quality of having good moral principles and behaving in a way that aligns with a set of positive traits. Virtue, not the outcome, defines the moral character of our actions.

The Stoic philosophy centers on four cardinal virtues: wisdom, justice, courage, and temperance. These virtues correspond to qualities like honesty, integrity, kindness, and prudence. When our actions align with these virtues, we are considered virtuous because these qualities lie within our control.

The Stoics encourage us to prioritize the cultivation of our inner virtues and character, rather than becoming overly preoccupied with external circumstances, many of which are beyond our control. This approach empowers us to lead purposeful and content lives. In the sections that follow, we will delve into these key principles and practical applications, exploring their relevance in the context of goal pursuit, adversity, and uncertainty.

Key Stoic Principles

> "Pay attention to your impressions, watch over them without sleeping, for what you guard is no small thing: self-respect and fidelity and self-possession, a mind free from emotion, pain, fear, disturbance – in a word, freedom." — Epictetus, Discourses

Now, let's explore some key Stoic principles that form the foundation of this philosophy:

Desire for Control

- **The desire for control is a cause of many problems:** This is why we should focus on what we can control. We can control our thoughts, actions, and judgments, but external events and the behaviors of others are beyond our control.

Examine Beliefs and Opinions

- **Examine your opinions, beliefs, and judgments:** Just like our desire for control, our beliefs and opinions cause us to misjudge situations as either good or bad. Misjudgments make us act impulsively, such as when we panic, stress over something, or feel the urge to act on a whim. Instead, we should understand that our immediate and visceral reactions are based on how we interpret events as good or bad and act accordingly. In light of that, we ought to continuously examine our opinions and beliefs to manage our emotions more effectively and make better judgments and decisions.

Live a Virtuous Life

- **Live a virtuous life:** To live a good, happy, and content life, we should live virtuously, according to the Stoics. Living in accordance with reason means that we are wise enough to manage our emotions and lead a life characterized by wisdom, courage, justice, and temperance. By developing the habit of living virtuously, we focus on our lives and decisions and what we can control, rather than what we can't control. More on these topics will be covered in the third part of the book.

The Four Cardinal Virtues

- **The Four Cardinal Virtues:** Stoicism identifies four cardinal virtues that guide ethical decision-making: wisdom (practical wisdom and knowledge), courage (moral courage in the face of adversity), justice (fairness and integrity), and temperance (self-control and moderation).

Understanding these foundational principles is essential as we delve into practical applications of Stoicism in the pursuit of our goals.

Practical Applications of Stoicism in Pursuit of Goals

Turning our attention to what we aspire to achieve, the Stoic approach offers valuable insights.

Avoid Attachment

- **Avoid becoming overly attached to wealth, status, or reputation:** Why? Because if you believe achieving them is inherently good, but you fail to attain, or lose, them, it will cause you unnecessary stress and distress.

> "He who gets excited about fame after death doesn't consider that anyone who remembers him will also die very soon, then again the one who succeeds that one, until all recollection has been extinguished by passing through a succession of people who foolishly admire and perish." — Marcus Aurelius

View Goals as Tools

- **View your goals as tools to promote the good rather than as ultimate ends:** Stoics advocate pursuing objectives that align with virtues like wisdom, courage, justice, and temperance. While you may aspire to attain success, wealth, or recognition, the Stoic perspective advises concentrating on these goals as chances for personal development and contributions to the greater good, rather than inherently good or bad outcomes.

> "He who has need of riches feels fear on their account. But no man enjoys a blessing that brings anxiety. He is always trying to add a little more. While he puzzles over increasing

his wealth, he forgets how to use it." — Seneca

Practice Humility

- **Practice humility and embrace the result:** As mentioned earlier, outcomes frequently do not mirror the quality of decisions or plans. This is why Stoicism emphasizes accepting the outcome and preserving humility to prevent falling into the trap of hubris. Sometimes things deviate from our plans, while other times our success surpasses our wildest expectations. In both scenarios, we should avoid becoming demotivated or overly complacent.

"The beginning of philosophy – at least for those who take hold of it in the right way, and through the front door – is an awareness of one's own weakness and incapacity when it comes to the most important things." — Epictetus

Attaining Tranquility and Contentment

- **The ultimate aim is to attain tranquility and contentment:** Living a good life, according to Stoicism, centers on achieving a state of inner tranquility and contentment. This entails recognizing that the only aspect you can control is your own actions. Thus, the objective is to nurture a virtuous and excellent character, striving to prepare for adversity. This state of tranquility and contentment isn't something you can merely check off a list; instead, it's an ongoing state that you must continually pursue, nurture, and uphold.

"If virtue promises good fortune, peace of mind, and happiness, certainly also the progress toward virtue is progress toward each of these things." — Epictetus

Practical Stoic Principles in Dealing with Adversity:

In a manner comparable to favorable events and outcomes, the Stoics had a similar approach to adversity. The following are some practical tips.

Negative Visualization and Premortem

- **Incorporate the practices of negative visualization and premortem into your decision-making toolkit:** The Stoics advocated a valuable approach to prepare for adverse events: mentally simulating the worst-case scenario. This doesn't mean dwelling on the negatives in every endeavor but rather exploring potential pitfalls along the way. By doing so, you equip yourself to proactively hedge against undesired outcomes to mitigate the impact.

"Begin the morning by saying to yourself: today I will meet with the busybody, the ungrateful, and the arrogant; with the deceitful, the envious, and the unsocial. All these things result from their not knowing what is good and what is evil. But I have seen the nature of the good – that it is beautiful; and the nature of evil, and that it is ugly; and the nature of him who does wrong, and that he is akin to me – not because he is from the same blood and seed, but because he partakes of the same mind and the same small bit of divinity. I cannot be injured by any of them, because no one can involve me in anything ugly except myself. And how can I be angry with my kin, or hateful towards them?" — Marcus Aurelius

Acceptance and Moving Forward

- **Accept the situation:** Accepting your fate or the situation is not the same as giving up and not doing anything about it. If you don't get the promotion for which you worked so hard, there isn't much you can do to reverse the situation at the moment.

  Zeno couldn't do anything to go back in time and prevent the shipwreck. If you launch a product that fails, there's little you can do to reverse that. According to the Stoics, if you practice negative visualizations and hedge for the worst-case scenario, there isn't much you can do to change the outcomes and events that lie outside of your control.

  As a result, the best thing you can do is to accept the situation and start thinking of ways to move forward. This forward-thinking mindset is essential to avoid falling into the trap of pessimism. It is crucial to acknowledge failure and think of new ways to improve the situation going forward.

  "We must learn to put up with what we cannot avoid. Our life, like the harmony of the world, is composed of contrary things – of diverse tones, sweet and harsh, sharp and flat, sprightly and solemn. The musician who only loved some of them – what would he be able to do? He has to know how to make use of them all, and be able to mix them together. We must do the same with the good and the bad, which are of the same substance as our lives." — Montaigne

Emotional Management

- **Manage your emotions to prevent negative consequences:** Managing emotions doesn't mean eradicating or negating them entirely. When someone insults you, you have the choice to either react impulsively or acknowledge the anger their insult may have provoked. Take a step back, count to 10, and consider a more effective way to deal with the situation. It's crucial to invest time in reflecting on your emotions, understanding their origins, and selecting a response that benefits you in the long term. This emotional detachment enables you to make more effective decisions.

"It is not what men do that disturbs us (for those acts are matters of their own control and reasoning), but our opinions of what they do. Take away those opinions – dismiss your judgment that this is something terrible – and your anger goes away as well." — Marcus Aurelius

Meditation and Self-Control

- **Practice meditation & self-control:** In the Stoic tradition, meditation and self-control play a significant role in maintaining inner tranquility in challenging situations. This involves resisting impulsive reactions and aligning decisions with long-term goals. Meditation, according to the Stoics, enhances self-awareness, emotional management, and mental clarity, contributing to resilience in the face of uncertainty and adversity.

"The character of those things you often think about will be the character of your understanding, for the mind is dyed by its thoughts. Dip it, therefore, in a succession of thoughts such as these: for instance, that where it is possible to live, it is also possible to live well." — Marcus Aurelius

Virtuous Response

- **Virtuous Response:** When confronted with adversity, ask yourself, "What virtue can I practice in this situation?" For example, facing challenges with courage, responding with wisdom, and maintaining patience during difficult times.

  "Our common life is founded on kindness and harmony; it is bound in a compact of mutual assistance, not by fear, but by love of one another." — Seneca

Stoicism is about being prepared

Stoicism is not about enduring pain or actively seeking hardships as a prerequisite for achieving greatness. It doesn't involve repressing emotions, eradicating desires, or avoiding risks. It's not about stressing over wealth, avoiding it, or living an ascetic life in isolation from society. Nor is it about complacently accepting the hand you've been dealt and thinking you can't or shouldn't do anything about it.

Stoicism was developed to address issues like uncertainty and adversity, not by avoiding them altogether, but by equipping ourselves with the necessary tools and habits to prepare for and navigate them as smoothly as possible. Consequently, if I were to summarize Stoicism in one word, I would say it's about **preparation**.

For the Stoics, readiness is crucial when facing future uncertainty. It encompasses not only strategic elements, such as formulating multiple plans or diversifying your investment and career portfolio, but also involves physical fitness to prepare for old age, as well as psychological and mental preparation to prevent becoming prisoners to our emotions. Failure to manage our emotions can lead to impulsive actions, resulting in negative consequences and harm to both ourselves and others in the short and long term.

Reducing financial or career risk can be readily managed by diversifying your portfolio and income streams. As for minimizing the risk of disease and injuries as we age, hitting the gym and eating well is an effective approach. Yet, managing episodes of stress, sadness, fear, anger, or the myriad of emotions and desires that may overwhelm us presents a more challenging endeavor.

This was the very challenge that the Stoics wrestled with. Even in a hypothetical scenario where Zeno had all his business insured and managed to salvage some money from it, he might still have been left with deep psychological scars. Similarly, whether you're coping with the loss of a loved one, job termination, a business failure, an insufferable micromanaging boss lacking self-awareness, or challenging interactions with colleagues or employees, the Stoics' teachings offer valuable guidance.

However, the intention isn't to passively accept and endure suffering. By contemplating the worst-case scenario, even though you may never fully grasp its emotional impact, you can simulate and mentally rehearse what it's like to undergo a comparable situation. This enables you to manage things as effectively as possible, reducing or alleviating potential harm.

To take an extreme but relatable example, if you're a Formula 1 driver or involved in any other fast car racing, although you don't want to be involved in a crash, it's still beneficial to contemplate the worst-case scenario (negative visualization). This prepares you mentally and physically to minimize the risk and potential damages.

Cultivating this contemplative habit will make it easier for you to act 'reasonably' based on all the internalized processes and steps to take in the event of a crash, even in a split second. This includes decisions such as whether to release your hands from the steering wheel or how to quickly exit the car, among other things.

As I considered examples for this chapter, I did a quick Google search for movies featuring Stoic characters. The results were quite interesting and reflected the common understanding people have about Stoicism. The movies I found, which prominently showcase Stoic characters, included The Shawshank Redemption, Bridge of Spies, Lawrence of Arabia, and Equilibrium.

You don't have to know the movies to grasp their essence. Specifically, they depict situations in which the protagonists endure extreme adversity and heroically navigate them while maintaining composure, to some extent.

These movies indeed offer a suitable example and significant inspiration if you're in the process of cultivating a Stoic mindset. Nevertheless, using these extreme cases as a reference may cause you to underestimate or discard the frustration, anger, and stress you encounter daily at work, on the road, or at home.

The nature of adversity and future uncertainty varies depending on the context. For instance, if you're in Silicon Valley, the specific challenges you face may differ from those encountered by someone building a startup in a region lacking Silicon Valley's infrastructure and network.

Similarly, if you live in a country with a relatively safe and stable environment, uncertainty and adversity will manifest differently compared to living in a troubled country plagued by war, inflation, economic crises, and virtually no prospects. And if you are not building a business, your worst-case scenario is not the same as that of Zeno's.

Rather than relying on movie examples, I opted to include three brief illustrations: two from business leaders I interviewed for this book and one from my personal experience.

Hassan builds on the side

Hassan Osman enjoys his day job in the tech industry. He graduated as a Civil Engineer and started his career as a tech consultant, steadily advancing within the company, changing countries, firms, and positions until he became a VP at a leading IT services firm. In hindsight, Hassan's career path seems to have been linear, steady, and almost certain, but he never took that for granted. Despite his comfortable jobs, Hassan consistently considered the worst-case scenario: getting laid off for any reason whatsoever.

Rather than deceiving himself into believing he was an exceptional employee and dismissing this possibility, Hassan decided to take action and prepare for the eventuality of a job loss. Consequently, he slowly but steadily began building on the side. After work each day, he dedicated 2 or 3 hours to either writing practical books addressing workplace problems or creating courses to help others effectively tackle these issues.

The results took time to accumulate but have compounded over time. As of today, Hassan has published 18 short and practical books with over 92k readers and developed 12 courses on Udemy with over 300k students. While he could comfortably sustain himself from the products he sells and the speaking opportunities he receives, Hassan still enjoys his day job. Hence, his brand now emphasizes that everything he creates is 'on the side,' and encourages others to do the same (a modern-day Stoic if you ask me.)

Rather than fixating excessively on the potential negative consequences of losing his job, Hassan embraced a Stoic mindset and diversified his income streams by building a portfolio, thereby hedging against any financial or emotional challenges he might encounter in the worst-case scenario.

Peter hedges against layoffs

Peter Askew experienced more layoffs than he could count, often facing unfulfilled promises of job positions. However, instead of sinking into a whirlpool of anxiety, frustration, and anger, Peter chose to embrace adversity. He envisioned himself being laid off as soon as he started a new job, a continuous negative visualization that drove him to acquire a diverse set of skills in each position he held. Like Hassan, he used these skills to develop a side business.

During this period, the internet remained a largely uncharted territory. Fascinated by the online world, Peter took it upon himself to learn website building, online marketing techniques such as ads and SEO, and monetization through ads. Over time, he also recognized the crucial role of acquiring excellent domain names as a foundation for successful businesses.

Through a series of trials and errors, Peter eventually mastered these aspects and gained enough momentum to leave his full-time job. He has since devoted himself to building businesses by acquiring expired domain names that inspired his entrepreneurial ventures.

One such venture began when he unexpectedly won a bid for the expiring domain name vidaliaonions.com. He hadn't anticipated winning the bid, but he did. Fortunately, he lived just a few hours away from the Vidalia region, where these onions are cultivated.

Due to their mild and sweet flavor, this particular onion variety has been granted a Protected Geographical Indication status, signifying that only onions grown in Vidalia can bear this label. As a result, Peter ended up partnering with a Vidalia farmer and has been selling Vidalia onions on the vidaliaonions.com website he developed since February 2015.

Without knowing it, Peter's Stoic mindset involved mentally and strategically preparing for yet another layoff. Not only did he practice negative visualization, but he also took the necessary measures to improve his situation and become less dependent on the market's whims.

He continues to embrace this mindset by concurrently developing multiple projects, constantly refining his skills, and guarding against potential pitfalls that may arise from unexpected forces like economic downturns or potential weather-related crop damage.

Another aspect where Peter unknowingly applies Stoicism is in his customer support, consistently managing his emotions to address customer problems in the fairest possible manner.

How adopting a Stoic mindset helped me navigate adversity

I've already shared my story in the introduction to this book, so I won't go over it in detail again. I'm more interested in showing how adopting a Stoic mindset, which is certainly not an easy task, helped me navigate professional and personal adversity and uncertainty.

I will focus on two interrelated aspects: career and economic. Over the span of seven years in academia, I gradually experienced mounting feelings of frustration, anger, stress, and anxiety due to the precariousness of my job situation.

During these seven years, I believed I had earned the right to be offered a permanent role at any of the universities where I was teaching in Lebanon. After all, I possessed all the necessary prerequisites, including a PhD, teaching experience, and some publications.

However, this never materialized into a full-time position. As the years went by, I became more resentful because, in my mind, not securing a steady job was a terrible thing. I was judging external events over which I had no control as bad things happening to me.

It's not that I wasn't trying to do anything about it; I anxiously yet eagerly attempted to find an industry job without any success. I was viewing my situation through a negative lens, lacking mental clarity, clouded by an array of beliefs that were preventing me from taking the proper actions to change my situation. I was stuck in a vicious circle.

While I was earning good money from two part-time gigs and gaining a great deal of experience in dealing with uncertainty by increasing my income streams, I nevertheless chose to focus on what I did not have because I thought it was bad not to have a permanent position.

During that time, I even managed to save some money on the side. Not much, just enough to sustain me for six months if I had lost my job. Yet, I was stressed and depressed. I even began to resent philosophy and was not investing in myself, even though I could have acquired new skills or established contact with a different network to transition from academia.

When I started teaching the Stoics, whom I hadn't paid much attention to before, my perspective slowly began to change. This transformation commenced around 2018. Thankfully, during this time between 2018 and 2020, I engaged in serious introspection and took the time to focus on where I was and what I needed to do to enhance my skills to find a new path. Whereas I once felt a sense of entitlement, I understood that there was little I could do about the decisions other people made, and all I could control were my own actions. I decided to embark on a journey, a quest, hence my Twitter handle @decafquest. Long story short, by 2020, I had worked through my anger and frustration and was psychologically closer to a Stoic mindset than ever before.

Why is this an important detail? During the last couple of months of 2019 and the first few months of 2020, Lebanon experienced a severe economic crisis. During this period, I lost around 60% of my savings, and my salary devalued significantly. It went from the equivalent of $4,000 USD a month (this amount always fluctuated depending on the number of courses I was teaching each semester) to around $1,000 USD a month; now it would be worth much less. On top of all that, in March 2020 the entire world shut down, and we found ourselves in what seemed like a never-ending lockdown.

In absolute terms, this situation was infinitely worse than not getting a full-time position as a philosophy professor. Despite that, thanks to two years of Stoic habituation, I had cultivated a different mindset, one that enabled me to weather this storm.

Instead of lamenting the situation I found myself in, I accepted that there was little I could do to regain my savings and focused on ways to increase my income streams. Without the burden of unnecessary emotions, I found myself exploring new avenues and opportunities because I was not constrained by any defined set of beliefs. I remained open to new possibilities and began to see opportunities where I wouldn't have noticed any before.

That was when I decided to post a Tweet (now X) in which I announced my intention to offer an Existentialism in Literature course starting in June 2020. Unexpectedly, many people expressed their interest and signed up.

Through the subsequent help and endorsement of numerous individuals on social media, for whom I will always be thankful, including Nassim Nicholas Taleb, Daniel Vassallo, and Dan Azzi, I managed to reach a wider audience, which resulted in an increase in the number of sign-ups in the subsequent months. I could delve into this experience further, but I have already written about it elsewhere[8].

The point here is to contrast my situation pre and post-pandemic and economic crises in Lebanon. It was thanks to the Stoic mindset I had slowly cultivated that I managed to stay afloat during a very rough period I lived through. I don't even want to imagine how bad my

---

[8]   https://link.medium.com/TJkjPfSouEb

reaction would have been, how angry and frustrated I would have become if I had not broken free from the vicious circle of stress in which I was trapped.

My lesson has been that Stoicism is not about eliminating life's uncertainties but equipping ourselves with the mental and emotional tools to address them as effectively as possible.

For me, Stoicism revolves around maintaining control over our judgments and beliefs. It's about habituating and training ourselves to simulate worst-case scenarios not to dwell on how dire things could become, but to open up a world of possibilities and opportunities that can minimize the impact of uncertainty and adversity.

Concluding Remarks

There are only a handful of things of which we might be certain in our lives. For instance, we can be certain, based on their definitions, that a triangle has three sides and that a bachelor is an unmarried man. There are also a few subject matters where, even if we're not 100% certain, a high degree of certainty can still be attained, and it's essential for us to be able to move forward without risking everyone's life.

Consider high-stakes endeavors like designing a reliable airplane, constructing a sturdy building, or engineering a safe and efficient car. In these pursuits, there is always a calculated risk that is meticulously accounted for. However, within the boundaries of the laws of physics, and with the use of quality materials and rigorous engineering, we can be reasonably certain that a building will not collapse, a plane will safely transport its passengers, and a car will function as intended. We don't want to be playing Russian roulette with our lives.

Nevertheless, even in these domains, entropy eventually takes its toll over time. Continuous maintenance and care are necessary to mitigate and manage depreciation to the best of our abilities. Thus, an element of uncertainty persists, reminding us that the world is inherently unpredictable.

Maybe the only certainty that looms over us is the inescapable fact of our mortality. Despite advancements in technology and medical science, the inevitability of death remains unchanged. We are beings toward death, as German philosopher Martin Heidegger puts it.

Given that there are only a few things of which we can be certain, uncertainty, adversity, and favorable events are fundamental aspects of the real world. It is for this reason that Stoicism places great emphasis on the importance of preparation.

In the realm of Stoic philosophy, preparation transcends physical and financial readiness. It also extends to the mental and psychological realms. Just as one prepares for the challenges of old age through physical training, such as regular gym workouts or engaging in challenging hikes, Stoics also aim to prepare themselves mentally through philosophical exercises and adequate mental models to anticipate and be ready for all sorts of potential business setbacks or natural occurrences by adopting a proactive mindset.

When it comes to preparing for possible business setbacks, a Stoic employs strategic thinking to anticipate potential mishaps and takes steps to diversify their investments or ventures.

However, the Stoic approach discourages an excessive obsession with diversification for its own sake. Instead, the focus remains on making rational decisions that align with one's objectives while maintaining self-awareness about personal limitations.

It's essential to recognize, though, that Stoicism is not a one-time pursuit but an ongoing practice. Stoics understand the value of continuously keeping themselves in check, both mentally and emotionally, and of training themselves to confront any adversity that life may present. This unwavering commitment to self-improvement and effective management of emotions, desires, and affections forms the bedrock of Stoic philosophy, allowing individuals to navigate the unpredictable currents of existence with philosophical wisdom and emotional fortitude.

Chapter 6: The Quest for Meaning

"Man's Search for Meaning" is the primary motivation in his life and not a "secondary rationalization" of instinctual drives. This meaning is unique and specific in that it must and can be fulfilled by him alone; only then does it achieve a significance that will satisfy his own will to meaning." — Viktor Frankl

Chris Quits his Job

After leaving his well-paying finance job, Chris noticed his newfound free time to be anxiety-inducing. For the first time in many years, dating back to his college days, he had ample time for introspection.

He had always been a top performer, he tells me, aspiring to excel first in college and then in his job, continually climbing the promotion ladder for as long as possible. Professional progress seemed straightforward for him. Advancing through the ranks required effort, but combined with enough patience, he believed he would not only reach the top but also secure financial stability.

Chris initially welcomed this comforting sense of certainty. His life and career path appeared predetermined and nearly set in stone. Despite this, he had a lingering sense of unease, something that didn't quite feel right.

Chris came to the realization that he found neither satisfaction nor fulfillment in his work anymore. Over time, the value of his job diminished, and the once-assured paycheck and rank advancement no longer felt guaranteed. With a growing sense of discontent, disillusionment, and alienation, Chris made the bold choice to resign at the age of 40.

It was a well-calculated move. He had enough savings to support himself and his family for several years without any income. He had more than enough time to figure out what he wanted to do next, spend quality time with his family, and explore new opportunities— something he had not even considered before because finance had been his sole plan all along.

Upon leaving his job, Chris thought that with his skill set and experience, he would quickly find something more meaningful to do after a short sabbatical. Surprisingly, this sabbatical extended longer than he had expected or accounted for due to the COVID-19 outbreak. Uncertainty knocked at Chris' door and, for the first time, he welcomed it with open hands.

During that time, the deepening feelings of stress and anxiety Chris experienced were neither financial nor psychological but rather existential. The more time he had for introspection and exploring his interests, passions, and life goals, the more he realized that he had been on autopilot for as long as he could remember.

"Weekdays were for work, and weekends were for activities to disconnect from work," he told me. The activities he engaged in, including hikes and golfing, among others, were things he did to pass the time with friends and family—activities people typically did on weekends— rather than interests he genuinely wanted to undertake. However, now that he no longer had to 'escape work' or 'do activities because everyone was doing them,' he didn't know what he was interested in, what skills he needed to develop, or what activities he wanted to engage in.

Chris needed some time to adjust to the new situation. During this period, he engaged in some serious self-examination and explored various activities to identify and nurture new interests. He enrolled in online courses to refine and enhance his skills, started writing, shared his work on social media, even launched a newsletter, and began connecting with online communities.

This period of self-discovery, or more like rediscovery, helped Chris improve his sense of self-awareness and identify his strengths and weaknesses. He embraced uncertainty as a fundamental aspect of life and changed his mindset to accommodate it.

Instead of doubling down on one goal that almost gave no meaning to his work or life, Chris adopted a more diversified approach, building and engaging in various projects that held greater significance for him. This approach helped him establish a better work-life balance, spend more time with his family, pursue his interests, and grow both professionally and personally.

As Chris embarked on his journey of self-discovery, his experiences echoed a sentiment many of us may encounter. You may find Chris' story relatable because of that. You may have undergone a similar experience yourself. This feeling of angst, anxiety, and inexplicable inquietude may have overtaken you by surprise on a Sunday afternoon or night, commonly known as the Sunday blues.

Existential Vacuum and the Search for Meaning

This sentiment was examined in depth by Viktor Frankl (1905 — 1997), Austrian psychiatrist, neurologist, and philosopher who offers an antidote to it in his seminal work "Man's Search for Meaning." In the following, I will delve into some of the key aspects of Frankl's philosophy and discuss his development of logotherapy, a psychotherapeutic theory based on years of practice and his personal experiences enduring atrocities and suffering as a prisoner in the Nazi concentration camps.

Frankl refers to the feeling of emptiness we experience as an existential vacuum, irrespective of the scale and magnitude of the experience. An existential vacuum in its most acute and ultimate manifestation results in what philosophers call an existential crisis.

According to Frankl and many other philosophers, who came to be known as existentialist philosophers, the existential vacuum emerges as a result of boredom, or the feeling of emptiness that we may occasionally experience during our lives.

These states are usually accompanied by feelings of anxiety, stress, sadness, angst, and unease. However, what makes these feelings more difficult to handle is that they are not caused by any direct tangible, and concrete event or encounter. Instead, they result from a vacuum or the absence of something. Frankl attributes this feeling to the absence of meaning in our lives.

A minor case of Sunday blues may be easy to deal with and may not push us to examine the reasons behind it. Some of the more common explanations given for this phenomenon are that we dread going back to work and what this signifies as the end of the weekend, marking the beginning of a new accelerated workweek full of stress and other problems. However, Viktor Frankl frames this problem, which he refers to as the 'Sunday neurosis,' differently.

According to Frankl, the reason we experience Sunday blues is that, during these few hours when we are doing nothing, resting, and preparing for Monday, we are overwhelmed by sensations of boredom. Unconsciously, we react to the emptiness in our lives, which is less apparent during the hustle and bustle of the week, but becomes more acute on a calm Sunday evening.

In a way, this anxiety isn't caused by the stressful work environment but by the absence of that noise, leaving us with little to nothing that could be considered meaningful. That's what Chris' experience consisted of. He realized he had spent his entire life chasing goals that stopped being meaningful for him. The way he solved this problem was by taking a step back and spending some time to figure out what would constitute experiences that gave more meaning to his existence.

Frankl warns that there is no universal formula to finding meaning in life. In other words, what worked for Chris may not work for you or others. More on this shortly.

According to Frankl, human beings are not primarily driven by a will to power or a will to pleasure, as some philosophers and psychoanalysts suggest.

Instead, Frankl contends that we are mainly motivated by a profound desire for meaning. When this longing for meaning is frustrated, it gives rise to an existential vacuum, which often leads to distress. Unfortunately, this distress tends to be mistakenly mitigated by the pursuit of pleasure or power.

This is why Frankl developed a new theory he called *logotherapy*, which served as the foundation for his psychiatric and psychotherapeutic practice. *Logotherapy*, as he explains, relies on existential analysis to assist individuals in identifying the root of their existential crisis, which exacerbates their existential vacuum. It helps them explore activities and experiences that can instill a fresh sense of meaning in their lives.

Frankl elaborates that the logotherapist, much like Socrates, doesn't impose a specific solution on people but instead aids in broadening their perspective to consider a wide array of available options that can bring greater meaning to their lives.

We should, therefore, attempt to find our own meaning in life, because if we don't, we would either want to become like other people—conformists—or we would be prone to do what other people wish us to do—totalitarianism. Chances are, many of us may have fallen into both of these traps at one point or another in our lives.

Combating Existential Vacuum

To remedy this, Frankl suggests three ways through which we can discover and create meaning in our lives:

1. **Creative values:** Creating a work or doing a deed.
2. **Experiential values:** Experiencing goodness, truth, beauty, nature, culture, or connecting with someone in a unique way through acts of love.
3. **Attitudinal values:** Adopting an adequate attitude toward unavoidable suffering, akin to ancient Stoicism.

The next time you experience an episode of Sunday blues, ask yourself this question: What have I been doing over the past few weeks, months, or years that have been giving my life more meaning? Depending on your answer, your goal would be either to figure out a way to engage in more meaningful activities or to seek new ones.

In one example that Frankl shares, a high-ranking American diplomat visited his Vienna office to continue the psychoanalysis sessions he had begun in New York, which had been going on for five years. The first question Frankl asked him was why he believed he should undergo analysis. It became clear that the diplomat was dissatisfied with his job, skeptical, and was finding it difficult to comply with American foreign policy.

His previous analyst suggested that the source of his discontentment wasn't so much the job itself but rather what working for the government symbolized for him. He was led to believe that his issue with authority would be resolved by reconciling with his father because the government and his bosses resembled father figures to him. This was not an interpretation Frankl found convincing.

Instead, after a series of interviews echoing Socratic dialogues, Frankl assisted the diplomat in identifying the source of his frustration: the lack of meaning in his vocation. The job simply didn't hold much meaning for him. Consequently, he decided to change careers and pursue something that infused more meaning into his life. Five years later, when Frankl checked in with him, the former diplomat reported being extremely happy and content in his new job.

Based on what was previously mentioned, it's essential to keep a few things in mind:

1. There is no one-size-fits-all solution to existential problems.
2. Self-awareness, self-examination, and engaging in dialogue with others are crucial initial steps in determining meaningful pursuits.
3. Ask yourself whether your current actions are self-motivated, imposed upon you, or simply conforming to external expectations.
4. Living authentically entails aligning your actions with what you believe provides meaningful experiences, even in the face of adversity and uncertainty.

In other words, your lifestyle choices and career decisions do not matter as long as you're leading a life you find meaningful. For example, some may discover meaning in a 9 to 5 job, while others may seek it in a more entrepreneurial setup. It's also crucial to identify the source of discontent if you're unhappy with your current lifestyle. Could it be that you're dissatisfied with your job, similar to the diplomat's experience, or perhaps it's the 9 to 5 structure itself that doesn't align with your sense of fulfillment?

Moreover, and perhaps more importantly, according to Frankl, the pursuit of meaning and its creation is not a 24/7 endeavor. Frankl recognizes the complexity of life, which includes routines, duties, and tedious tasks that may not exactly be to our liking. However, the essence of *logotherapy* lies in urging us to make a conscious effort to engage in activities that offer greater value and meaning. This, in turn, allows us to strike a balance between meaningful and routine activities.

That said, let's take a closer look, accompanied by concrete examples, at the three values — creative, experiential, and attitudinal — proposed by Frankl for searching for, and creating more, meaning in life and combating the existential vacuum.

Attitudinal value: Finding meaning in suffering

We have already seen how the Stoics responded to adversity and uncertainty. The most important aspects of Stoicism involve preparing for uncertainty and adversity through meditation and negative visualization and managing emotions to effectively and reasonably deal with problems instead of getting caught in an endless whirlpool of negative sentiments.

I also mentioned that I preferred not to focus on extreme cases as examples of Stoicism as often depicted in some movies. Instead, my interest lay in addressing the more trivial problems we encounter on a daily basis and exploring how Stoicism could help us navigate through these situations. Another reason why I avoided using extreme fictional examples is that Viktor Frankl personally went through something much worse, which he utilized, along with his experience as a practicing psychiatrist, to develop his *logotherapy* theory.

In 1942, Frankl was arrested by the Nazis and transported to several concentration camps, including Auschwitz and Dachau. Over a span of three years, he endured the suffering, horror, and atrocities of the concentration camps, tragically losing his parents and his wife. To the best of his ability, Frankl was determined to survive and endeavored to provide psychiatric and medical assistance to the other prisoners.

In addition to carrying out intense labor, he worked diligently to prevent suicides, conducted open and mass therapeutic sessions for those he shared a cell with, and offered medical assistance to typhoid patients until his liberation in 1945. These experiences played a crucial role in shaping his psychotherapeutic approach, *logotherapy*, which highlights the importance of finding meaning in life, even in the face of great adversity.

Frankl explained that in an extreme case of adversity and suffering, such as a concentration camp, the primary factor that sustained him and others was the continuous pursuit of meaning despite the immense suffering. He observed that even in the face of intense mental and physical pain, those who could turn inward and engage in inner exploration managed to endure suffering better than others with a stronger constitution but lacking that inner enrichment.

Frankl elaborated on how some inmates, who mentally resigned themselves to the harshness of their circumstances, would often pass away due to exhaustion. The primary remedy for this predicament, he assured, was to discover meaning amidst the suffering and, importantly, to help fellow inmates uncover their own sense of purpose.

According to Frankl, the first step towards this was to acknowledge the present and the suffering within it. In the harsh and uncertain conditions of concentration camps, he cautioned against dwelling on the past or becoming stuck in retrospective thoughts to avoid the present and render it unreal. By doing so, prisoners overlooked small opportunities to find meaning in the present, and as a result, they were unable to imagine a near or distant future with a goal or purpose that could infuse meaning into their existence.

As such, to endure such extreme hardship, Frankl presented several ways to find meaning in suffering:

1. **Acknowledging and accepting unavoidable suffering:** First and foremost, it is important to keep in mind that Frankl does not believe suffering is necessary for one to live a meaningful life. He asserts that if suffering is avoidable, then one should find ways to alleviate it.

   Frankl's view is that when suffering is unavoidable and lies beyond one's control, the best response is to acknowledge and accept it. This, of course, is not an easy task and requires significant mental and psychological effort. However, according to Frankl, in alignment with Stoic philosophy, choosing how to respond to such harsh conditions can make the suffering more bearable.

   By accepting unavoidable suffering, Frankl maintains, we free ourselves from the cycle of despair and the process of finding a reason why such a thing is happening to us and whether or not we deserve it.

   Instead, we would be better prepared to confront the arbitrariness of life by finding the inner strength to keep going. It was this attitude that helped him and his fellow inmates persevere.

   In Frankl's own words: *"When a man finds that it is his destiny to suffer, he will have to accept his suffering as his task; his single and unique task. He will have to acknowledge the fact that even in suffering he is unique and alone in the universe. No one can relieve him of his suffering or suffer in his place. His unique opportunity lies in the way in which he bears his burden."*

2. **Finding meaning in small moments:** When one accepts suffering and acknowledges the present, it becomes easier to

identify small positive moments within it. For Frankl and the inmates, these brief instances made the suffering more bearable. Examples included exchanging kind words with fellow prisoners or being assigned to the line where the cook distributed soup equally among all inmates without favoritism. In these occasional meager pleasures and small moments, Frankl found meaning that made the suffering more bearable.

3. **Maintaining a goal or a sense of purpose:** Frankl explains that one peculiar aspect of human beings is that we can only live toward the future. If we get stuck in retrospective thoughts without using those as an opportunity to propel ourselves into the future, we would be implicitly giving up hope in life. It is essential to find meaning in adversity and suffering by maintaining a sense of goal or purpose. In the case of Frankl, it was the determination to complete the manuscript he was working on, and which he was forced to surrender upon being taken as prisoner.

   On occasions, he would even imagine himself giving a lecture about the psychology of concentration camps, and this would help him transcend his immediate suffering and reframe it as though it was a thing of the past.

   In the case of other prisoners who had contemplated suicide, Frankl encouraged them to think about something or someone that could provide a sense of purpose to continue living.

   For one prisoner, it was his beloved child who was safe in a foreign country, while for another, a scientist, it was the unfinished book series he had started before his arrest.

Faced with unavoidable suffering and hardship, Frankl emphasizes that the pursuit of meaning is paramount for endurance as human beings inherently live toward the future. While adversity and uncertainty may distort our perception of the future, seeking meaning helps shift our focus away from dwelling on the past and directs us toward a forward-oriented perspective.

The objective is not to seek happiness in such challenging circumstances, nor to rationalize an otherwise absurd and random occurrence. Instead, the goal is to persist by embracing the situation, cherishing small moments of significance, and discovering a purpose that ignites one's determination to keep going.

Experiential value: finding meaning in beautiful experiences

Another way to combat existential vacuum and boredom, in addition to finding meaning in unavoidable suffering, is to find meaning in beautiful experiences. This applies both to personal and professional life.

What does this actually mean? First, think about the activities you undertake and all the experiences you gain. These may include participating in networking events, connecting with online communities, going on a Sunday hike with your work colleagues or friends, engaging in team-building activities, visiting museums with your family and friends, going to the movies, and reading books, among others.

The main drive to carry out such activities may differ depending on the context. You may participate in these activities as part of your work, career development, and advancement. It could also be for building relationships with colleagues, family, or new friends. Perhaps you are engaging in these activities because they are on your bucket list or because they align with social norms and you want to fit in. Maybe it's because you believe it's essential to cultivate an aesthetic sensibility, which is why you visit the Louvre or the Prado, or because you wish to share content on your social media pages, brag about the places you've visited, or simply because you're following a social media trend.

Frankl warns against falling into the traps of totalitarianism or conformism because, in both cases, we are at risk of experiencing an exacerbated sense of existential vacuum, dread, and angst. If all the activities we pursue lack any sense of meaning for us, then sooner or later, they become an escape from reality or noise that we subject ourselves to just to avoid the feelings of despair arising from the inexplicable feeling of boredom that overwhelms us. Think again of the Sunday blues.

The antidote? In a complex life where a lot of things fall outside your control, with duties you have to attend to, and many professional and personal commitments stack up your calendar, the key, Frankl suggests, is in pursuing some activities and experiences that you find meaningful.

Chris managed to do that by quitting his job and taking some time to reflect on what really made him tick. However, as I already pointed out earlier, there is no one-size-fits-all solution to the question of meaning. For instance, you may not be able to quit or change jobs for a variety of reasons. Your calendar may be busy for reasons beyond your control.

The question remains: What experiences do you think you could pursue that would be meaningful for you? These could include, as Frankl affirms, loving someone, building meaningful relationships with your friends, establishing meaningful connections with your colleagues, and experiencing something beautiful like watching a sunset, listening to music, or contemplating beautiful art, and having a nice meal among others. This experience of the beautiful is what is referred to in philosophy as aesthetic experience.

Aesthetic experiences are the result of encountering an event, object, or activity that evokes a profound sensory and emotional response, extending beyond mere pleasure. These encounters often prompt a heightened sense of appreciation, beauty, or significance, transcending the ordinary and connecting us with a deeper understanding of our own sensibilities.

This experiential value that Frankl talks about doesn't only have to be limited to aesthetic experiences, or experiences of beauty. They can be as simple as creating meaningful connections with friends or colleagues. So next time you are at a networking event, maybe try to establish meaningful connections instead of racing against time to make sure everyone gets your business card.

What constitutes meaningful experiences, such as moments of beauty, strong relationships, or engaging conversations, for you? You don't necessarily have to visit a museum, for instance, to have an aesthetic experience. Perhaps you find museums dull and believe they don't offer genuinely meaningful experiences. Therefore, if you aren't required to visit a museum for work purposes, why would you bother with the trouble?

Of course, this may take us down the route of what beauty is and whether aesthetic taste is subjective or objective. But I won't dwell on this or take up this task here because it is beside the point.

The main idea behind all this is that oftentimes we are drowned in mundane activities and forget what we like, what our interests are, and which beautiful experiences give meaning to our lives. Instead, we let ourselves operate on autopilot, doing things that may not really be meaningful to us just because everyone else is doing them.

A wonderful movie that captures Viktor Frankl's suggestion regarding the pursuit of meaning through beautiful experiences is "The Great Beauty," directed by Paolo Sorrentino.

On his 65th birthday, the protagonist, Jep Gambardella, a disillusioned writer and journalist, confronts an existential crisis. He settled in the historically rich and beautiful city of Rome during his youth, and his first novel catapulted him to fame and fortune. His home boasted a view of the Coliseum, and he enjoyed leisurely walks through the historic streets of Rome, spent nights at lively parties, and often slept during the day. His social circle was small, comprised of friends from diverse backgrounds, including socialites, politicians, academics, and playwrights, with whom he occasionally shared dinners and conversations.

Yet, he grappled with an existential dread that led him to rethink his life and what he had experienced. Trying to bring together the old and the new, the meaningful and the banal, Jep began a journey of self-discovery in search of purpose, beauty, and meaning.

Instead of capturing 'the great beauty,' he realized that beauty and meaning were to be found in the small things and experiences in life. Jep reconnected with his past in an introspective process that led to greater self-awareness about his superficial, banal, and meaningless behavior and practices.

Jep started to develop deeper and more genuine connections with his friends. He began to appreciate the contrasting beauty of Rome, embracing both the modern aspects of life and the historical backdrop of ancient and beautiful architecture that defines the city. Additionally, he confronted his own mortality and discovered a fresh sense of purpose through a new project that helped him overcome his writer's block.

I don't want to delve further into the movie or Jep's character. What makes it interesting is how it reflects Frankl's idea of finding meaning through experiences to combat existential despair. You see, from an external perspective, it might seem like Jep had it all – good health, wealth, status, and friends. However, deep down, he was unsatisfied. He wasn't necessarily unhappy, but there was an underlying restlessness. What truly mattered, as he underwent his transformative and introspective journey, was not the number of activities he carried out or the mere fact that he was doing things; what mattered most was finding meaning in some of those activities.

Through this, he managed to find a sense of peace in the face of his own mortality and to strengthen his bonds with friends. He stopped chasing ideal moments, accepted his present and his past, and learned to appreciate the little things in life as long as they held meaning.

Beauty, aesthetic experiences, meaning, and purpose don't always have to be grandiose or extravagant moments we relentlessly pursue. They can also be found in simple, everyday encounters – a walk in nature, a friendly chat with a colleague, or a casual football match. These moments offer valuable insights into our own identities, and our preferences, and grant us a heightened sense of appreciation and perspective in the world.

Creative value: finding meaning in creativity

We have thus far seen two of the three ways to combat boredom and existential vacuum as proposed by Viktor Frankl, namely, finding meaning in unavoidable suffering and finding meaning in experiences and activities we explore like appreciating beauty, building authentic relationships, and loving someone.

The third remedy is creative value, or finding meaning in creativity and creative endeavors we undertake. This includes writing a book, creating an art piece, making music, writing a newsletter, starting your own business, writing code, and any other creative act you're interested in. In this section, I will examine this more closely, and I will be doing so by introducing Existentialism, which is more of a philosophical mode of inquiry. More on this shortly.

So far in this chapter, I have been exploring Viktor Frankl's analysis of the existential condition of human beings. As we saw, Frankl asserts that fundamentally humans are governed by the desire to find meaning. In order to move forward in life, combat boredom, and achieve a sense of quietude and satisfaction, we ought to dwell on an important question.

Instead of asking what the meaning of life is, which is more generic, abstract, and implies that there's one answer when in fact the answer is relative to each and every one of us, Frankl says that it is us that are being asked by life what the meaning of our existence is.

There isn't only one answer to that either. The meaning of our existence changes depending on the activities we pursue, and the circumstances we find ourselves in. So my question for you is, what is the meaning of your existence at the present moment?

Throughout this chapter, I've been using terms like existential analysis, existential vacuum, existential despair, dread, boredom and so on, but I've only shed light on these terms within the context of Frankl's psychotherapeutic theory *logotherapy* and his book "Man's Search for Meaning." The common word here is existence.

Frankl's concern with human existence and his attempts to help people combat existential vacuum and the loss of meaning by building the courage to find meaning and live a full life, even when going through unavoidable suffering, is one of the main characteristics of a philosophical movement, or a philosophical way of doing things, which came to be referred to and known as Existentialism.

Existentialism

Unlike Stoicism, Skepticism, Platonism, Aristotelianism, and other -isms, which are schools of philosophy with clear principles and distinct beliefs, worldviews, and perspectives, Existentialism isn't a philosophical school in the same sense. Instead, it's a way of doing philosophy that existentialist philosophers engage in. The main focus of existentialist philosophers is human existence, exploring what defines human beings, their fears, anxieties, aspirations, and how to navigate life in a seemingly meaningless universe.

Existentialist philosophy is more of a blanket term to refer to the kinds of themes that philosophers are interested in, rather than their thoughts on these themes. It's quite common to find existentialist philosophers who believe in God, such as the Danish philosopher Søren Kierkegaard, often seen as one of the early precursors of existentialism, or philosophers who are atheists, like the French philosopher Jean-Paul Sartre.

As such, Existentialism was more of an anti-systematic movement that wasn't so much concerned with abstract ideas but was more focused on the concrete individual, the human being of flesh and blood, as Spanish existentialist philosopher Miguel de Unamuno put it.

Viktor Frankl is considered an existentialist philosopher as well; he tackled the question of existence and meaning not abstractly but in a concrete sense as it relates to each person. We shouldn't ask ourselves what the meaning of life is but rather consider that the universe asks us what the meaning of our existence is.

I won't delve into the history of Existentialism or what it was a reaction against. However, if you're interested in the topic, you can check out William Barrett's compelling book "Irrational Man," where he contextualizes and lays out the foundation of Existentialism.

One thing I do want to highlight, though, is that some scholars and philosophers trace Existentialism all the way back to Socrates, one of the early philosophers who was more concerned with how human beings ought to live than with only asking questions about the nature of reality and the universe.

Existentialism as a movement became popular and resonated with many people, primarily in continental Europe and later in the United States. This popularity arose in the aftermath of the First World War but especially in the wake of the Second World War.

I will attempt to paint a picture to depict the ups and downs that people experienced during the first half of the 20th century and invite you to consider if you have personally encountered any of these experiences and how they might have affected you.

Imagine living in an era of a thriving economy and peaceful times, with promises of a great future where science would eventually answer life's most significant questions. This optimism stemmed from the significant strides humanity had taken over the past few centuries in developing tools and technology to understand reality, combat disease, and enhance the economy through more efficient transportation and streamlined production and commerce.

Life seemed promising, marked by an improved quality of life compared to medieval times, offering greater opportunities for making a decent living, gaining access to education, and securing apprenticeships.

However, on the other side, there was an impending economic crisis characterized by high inflation, market crashes, and rising unemployment, exacerbated by not one but two world wars. The same science that had promised to eradicate disease and foster human flourishing was now responsible for the creation of weapons, gas chambers, and atomic bombs.

One day, you might be enjoying a prosperous life, and the next, you find yourself on the streets, struggling for survival, surrounded by the stark realities of death and suffering. In such a grim context, you can't help but question the purpose of it all.

In short, this is why Existentialism became popular in the latter half of the 20th century. Of course, this is merely a simplified portrayal, and reality is far more intricate. Not everyone underwent the same experiences, and the impact of the wars differed between the United States and Europe.

However, the prevailing sentiment remained consistent: people initially harbored optimism about the future due to the promises of progress and thriving economies, only to be confronted with widespread destruction and suffering.

Philosophers began to realize that existence appeared fragile and absurd. Science, devoid of values and ethics, could inflict suffering, and philosophical discussions in the abstract about the world as a whole often overlooked the individual who had to endure this suffering.

Discussing humanism and our love for our fellow humans seemed somewhat abstract and absurd when neighbors were engaged in violence against each other. What was the point, ultimately? How should we confront death? What ethical responsibilities do we have towards each other as social beings? Should we prioritize defending our nation or staying behind to care for our parents? Are we truly free to choose? Do we bear moral and personal responsibility for the choices we make? How can we discover meaning in a universe that seems devoid of it?

These were some of the questions that existentialist philosophers grappled with. However, amidst all this doom and gloom, we've already seen how Frankl argues that we ought to find meaning in life despite the unavoidable suffering. So, while existentialist philosophers may differ in their outlook on life, they all generally agree that to make existence and our lives worth living, we must either find or create meaning, even in the face of uncertainty and adversity.

One way to combat the existential vacuum, despair, anxiety, and the absurdity of the universe is by creating something, as Frankl suggests. This creative endeavor should reflect our authentic selves. In other words, if we are to create something meaningful, it should align with our deep-seated desires. This is an important requirement for existentialists.

Often, when we experience an existential crisis, it's because we're not living the life we want, but rather the life that others have mapped out for us or expect us to live—whether it's society, employers, parents, or the community.

However, the goal of a meaningful existence is to live, to the best of our ability, in accordance with our true selves, doing what we are most passionate about, while avoiding the traps of conformity and totalitarianism, as Frankl explains.

Nausea

This quest for authenticity and creativity is beautifully explored in a novella written by French existentialist philosopher Jean-Paul Sartre called "Nausea," published in 1938. Sartre effectively articulates some of the existentialist themes we've discussed so far in a work of fiction that brings these ideas to life, making them relatable and understandable.

While Sartre did not particularly like the title suggested by the publisher, the term "nausea" in philosophical circles eventually acquired a new metaphysical meaning to describe the existential malaise we often experience, or as Frankl puts it, the existential vacuum. This nausea, encompassing inexplicable existential anxiety and angst in the face of death and the absurdity of existence, is difficult to articulate and explain, much like the feeling of Sunday blues.

In the novel, the nausea is experienced by the protagonist, Antoine Roquentin, who just can't seem to understand it. It isn't pathological or strictly psychological; rather, it's an overwhelming feeling that grips him as he roams the streets of Bouville, where he is staying to conduct historical research for writing the biography of an Aristocrat, the Marquis de Rollebon. Roquentin sits in a cafe, frequents the public library, and at some point, rests on a bench under a chestnut tree.

The novella essentially serves as Antoine Roquentin's journal, where he painstakingly documents his daily activities in the hope of capturing the essence of his nausea and making sense of it. Similar to Jep Gambardella from the previous section, Roquentin embarks on a journey of introspection, self-discovery, and personal growth.

He revisits his past experiences, loves, and adventures while reflecting on his recent thoughts, political beliefs, observations of the bourgeois in Bouville and their manners, and personal relationships. All of this is done in an attempt to identify the underlying cause of his metaphysical nausea and potentially find a cure.

As he delves into subjects like memory, history, and what constitutes an adventure, Roquentin begins to realize that he is not leading a meaningful and authentic life.

He recognizes that he has been running away from his own life by immersing himself in the life of a historical figure, the Marquis de Rollebon, whose life narrative he was trying to piece together based on archival material in the public library. This felt more like living vicariously for Roquentin; he was in Bouville only because the archival material was there. So, he was conditioned by something he was not truly interested in.

This is just one among the many epiphanies and experiences Roquentin has, including discussions with an autodidact man and encounters with his former lover, Anny. Eventually, Roquentin stops writing the biography of de Rollebon, decides to leave Bouville, and settles in Paris.

However, his primary awakening lies in the understanding that his inexplicable nausea was, in fact, his struggle with the absurdity, uncertainty, and meaninglessness that underlie human existence. Roquentin concludes that we are not predestined to fulfill a specific purpose; rather, we are free to choose to live authentically.

Yet, this freedom comes with the added burden of moral responsibility. Roquentin realizes that despite being conditioned by unchangeable circumstances, such as his birth to specific parents, as a redhead, in a certain year, he can still choose to live authentically and find his own meaning and purpose.

Roquentin's nausea seems to diminish when he listens to a song that would endure through time, long after the singer and the songwriter have passed away. So, he decides that he could give meaning to his life by cherishing the small, pleasant moments he experiences daily, including the beauty of music, and by writing a work of fiction.

Concluding remarks

Throughout this chapter, we have examined various solutions for existential crises caused by the existential vacuum from our encounters with uncertainty and adversity. One potential antidote, as we've explored, is to discover or cultivate meaning in our lives—whether in response to unavoidable suffering, through our experiences, or via our creative endeavors. So, the next time you find yourself grappling with an existential crisis, contemplate the actions you can take that hold personal significance for you.

However, whether in your professional or personal life your actions, experiences, and interactions come with a moral responsibility that can inform your choices, actions, and relations with others. Ultimately, we are social and communal beings. This topic—morality and moral responsibility—will be the focus of the third part of this book.

"In fact, freedom is in danger of degenerating into mere arbitrariness unless it is lived in terms of responsibility. That is why I recommend that the Statue of Liberty on the East Coast be supplemented by a Statue of Responsibility on the West Coast." — Viktor Frankl

III

Ethical decision-making frameworks

*"He is happy who lives in accordance with complete virtue
and is sufficiently equipped with external goods, not for some
chance period but throughout a complete life."* — *Aristotle*

Part Three: Introduction

I once moderated an online session that revolved around discussions about personal finance, investments, and entrepreneurship. During the session, I asked the guest a question that sparked concerns about the importance of ethics in the business world. The guest, wearing a smile, along with many attendees—most of whom were bankers and professionals—agreed that as long as actions are legal and compliant, there is no problem.

I chose to refrain from following up on my question and moved on to another, more 'practical' subject.

This was right around the GameStop short squeeze saga when a group of retail investors and Reddit users worked to drive up the stock price of struggling GameStop, resulting in substantial losses for hedge funds that had shorted the stock.

After gaining significant media attention, the event underwent thorough analysis in YouTube videos and documentaries, sparking conversations about market dynamics and regulations. These discussions aimed to address the need for preventative measures against similar social media-driven squeezes, even though such actions were not explicitly illegal.

Some of the arguments in the wake of this incident centered around the morality underlying such a practice. Discussions ensued about whether the coordinated efforts to increase the stock price were ethical. Some questioned the morality of the intention behind these efforts, which aimed to harm big investors and get rich quickly through a speculative mechanism.

In this particular case, I think that there's a high chance that ethics was invoked because those on the losing side had no legal recourse to rely on.

Advocates of the actions of retail investors and Redditors viewed it as a form of karmic, Robinhood-like, redistributive justice, with undertones reminiscent of the David vs. Goliath narrative. In this perspective, the perceived weaker but more deserving side triumphs over the 'bad' side.

But in the absence of regulatory measures and policies that prohibit such an undertaking, was it ethical or unethical? Does it even warrant or merit consideration from a moral perspective? What do you think?

I started this part with this example to emphasize how specific actions within the business and professional realm, while legally permissible, can still trigger considerable reflection and provoke extensive ethical debates.

In this case, your stance on whether stricter measures and regulations should be implemented to prevent another similar occurrence may be influenced by ethical considerations. You might feel uncomfortable with the idea of manipulating the market without violating the law.

Conversely, you might find it rewarding to hold large investment firms accountable for their reckless investment choices, with the hope that they would exercise greater caution in the future.

To defend any of these opposing standpoints, you would have to back your conclusion up with sound arguments that follow a coherent and logical structure and are built on true premises.

Here's the catch, though. If both arguments do make sense and are constructed based on rigorous reasoning and true premises, then why would we end up with contradictory and opposing conclusions? This is because, even if the facts and premises are true, the arguments laid out would rely on different ethical frameworks to examine and analyze the situation.

In the following chapters, my aim is not to suggest which ethical framework is superior or to provide definitive answers regarding the ethics of the GameStop affair, which I only used above to underscore the legal vs. ethical debate. Instead, my objective is to present three fundamental ethical frameworks that underpin all established legal, professional, and ethical principles and codes of conduct. The frameworks which will be discussed in detail are virtue ethics, consequentialism, and the theory of duty. The main objectives of this part are to:

1. Show you that you already use these frameworks in your day-to-day activities, even if you don't know it.
2. Provide you with the basic tools to carry out an ethical analysis.
3. Enable you to identify the different assumptions and frameworks underlying opposing arguments.

The ultimate goal is to help you realize that, more often than not, when we have disagreements regarding the ethics of a certain conduct or a particular issue, we are likely employing different frameworks.

By being able to identify these models, you will be better equipped to engage in more informed discussions and bridge the gap between opposing viewpoints, thus reducing unnecessary friction that tends to arise when discussing sensitive ethical topics.

From this point onward, for the sake of simplicity, I will use the terms "morality" and "ethics" interchangeably, even though there are some distinctions between the two. In philosophy, we typically do not emphasize these nuances, and unless you are pursuing advanced academic studies in ethics, distinguishing between them may not be crucial. Before we dig deeper into the crux of the different ethical decision-making frameworks, let us first quickly examine what ethics and morality are, and whether or not we should actually care about them.

Chapter 7: What is Ethics?

The simple answer to this big question is that no one really knows, to a certain extent. If you search for the definition of ethics, you are likely to come across answers that emphasize what ethics is not, or more specifically not reducible to, rather than providing a clear explanation of what ethics truly is.

A more straightforward yet vague answer would be that ethics is the branch of philosophy that deals with questions of right and wrong, and what sort of good behavior and decisions we ought to pursue to ensure that our conduct is ethical.

So far so good. We know that ethics and morality are concerned with right and wrong matters, and with how we ought to behave towards ourselves and others because we are social animals and live in communities and societies.

Great. However, a more immediate and intriguing yet complex question arises: How do we ascertain whether a conduct is morally right or wrong? And which actions, behaviors, and decisions belong to the realm of morality and ethics?

In other words, how can we determine whether an action should be evaluated from a moral perspective? For instance, is the debate over pineapple pizza a matter of morality, or is it more about subjective taste and preference? What about instances like lying to your friends, choosing one major over another, or deciding between job offers?

What specific criteria qualify an action for discussion and analysis from a moral and ethical standpoint? This is one reason why defining ethics can be exceedingly complex and delicate.

Here's another reason: human beings have, for a long time, drawn moral and ethical principles from a wide range of sources, including myths, religions, norms, conventions, philosophy, and law. What further complicates matters is that, at times, within the same group, moral dilemmas, debates, and contradictions arise due to differing stances between religion and the law, between norms, or as a result of different interpretations of a particular edict. Complexity deepens when individuals hold views that diverge from those of the entire group.

For example, when 'do not lie' and 'do not do harm' come into opposition, what would the best course of action be? This can apply to something as life-threatening as hiding an innocent person being unlawfully persecuted, or as insignificant as telling your friend a white lie.

This complexity exists not only within individual groups, societies, or countries but also on a global scale. In the global village, many people from diverse backgrounds interact and engage in business with one another on a daily basis. We work in international environments, constantly exposed to different, often opposing, perspectives and worldviews, moral or otherwise.

Some countries and societies rely primarily on religion as the source of their moral principles, which form the basis of their legal systems, while others draw from a combination of philosophy, law, and codes established and agreed upon by the international community.

You can sometimes observe the consequences of this on social media when intense and heated moral debates unfold concerning immigration, healthcare, and social welfare. However, these debates need not always focus on what might be considered serious matters; occasionally, the contention can be centered around seemingly casual topics, such as comedy.

At times, the discourse shifts towards the offense taken due to a comedian's joke, morphing the conversation toward what is morally acceptable to be the subject of comedy and jokes and what is not.

As a result, philosophers and researchers have long pondered the question of whether morality and ethics are subjective or objective, universal or relative. The study of the nature of morality and the scope of moral values falls under the branch of ethics called metaethics.

Can we assert that different cultures possess different moral codes, and therefore should we respect and refrain from interference if we believe they adhere to principles and practices we consider harmful and unethical? To give one example, think of bullfighting in Spain. This is sufficient to start a never-ending debate about ethics and traditions. You probably get the gist.

Where should we draw the line between merely pointing out that another culture's ethics are immoral and compelling them to cease their actions or change their principles and codes? And when two ethical systems collide, what would be the best course of action?

To provide a simple yet concrete example that underscores this issue, consider the difference in how various cultures perceive the exchange of gifts in a business setting.

In a Western context, this action has become frowned upon and is seen as a form of bribery, therefore being strictly prohibited by law. Meanwhile, in many non-Western countries, the exchange of gifts is an almost inherent and fundamental aspect of conducting business. So, who is right in this case? And what should be done in situations where a firm based in a Western country must do business with a firm based in a non-Western one? You're meeting your potential client over for lunch for the first time, what would you do?

I think it's becoming clearer why ethics and morality are not only challenging to define but also complex to contemplate, discuss, and analyze. However, our exploration isn't over yet! Another reason why this is a sensitive and intricate subject is because it permeates our lives, professions, and nearly everything we do, both on an individual and collective scale.

Ethics operates as a spectrum and a framework that becomes increasingly nuanced as we expand from individuals to families, communities, countries, and the entire world. Similarly, it gains complexity as we move across professions, from a small independent business to a family-run enterprise, to a small company, to a large corporation.

Moreover, the seriousness, risks, and potential harm resulting from our actions and decisions vary widely. For instance, telling a small white lie to a friend about the quality of the dinner they prepared may not lead to significant consequences. Using the office printer for personal use may not be particularly harmful either. Consuming someone's lunch at the office, as in Ross's case, might not have adverse consequences if your colleagues remain stoic about it.

However, issues like misrepresenting a product's safety, and debating topics that involve people's livelihoods such as money laundering, euthanasia, healthcare, and the ethics of war, involve a different level of gravity and complexity altogether.

Sometimes, disagreements and exchanges worsen because we are not mindful of these differences, and we don't take into consideration scale (an extremely interesting point Nassim Nicholas Taleb makes in "Antifragile" and elsewhere). Many times, this occurs due to mixing concepts and utilizing different ethical frameworks when analyzing a particular subject.

It is essential to keep all of that in mind when thinking about and discussing ethics and morality. I would also like to reiterate that in what follows I am not going to use extreme examples, nor am I going to suggest which of the proposed frameworks is better, if at all.

The main reason I mention all of this is to make you aware of the intricacy of the subject and to provide you with the basic and fundamental tools needed to increase your awareness of the field. This will make you better equipped to identify points of contention and the underlying assumptions that inform opposing arguments, helping you reflect on and discuss these issues with greater clarity.

A few more reasons why it's difficult to define ethics. Bear with me! Neither religion, nor the law, nor conventions are the primary source of ethics and morality. While they do contribute to the debate and inform some of the discussions, they don't necessarily reflect or represent a moral perspective, namely because morality evolves over time, and the law takes time to catch up, or vice versa.

For example, slavery was legal in many countries, even when many people considered it immoral. In the case of religion, the question becomes which of the religions has a better moral framework, and what does this entail for those who don't necessarily subscribe to any of these religions?

Given all the above, we can view ethics as a continuous effort to scrutinize our established principles, moral beliefs, and ethical behavior. This endeavor aims to ensure that both individually and collectively, we are striving to lead a virtuous and ethical life and treat one another well to the best of our abilities.

It's essential to remember that our standards of right and wrong, whether they find expression in the law, societal norms, or religious principles, fundamentally originate from ethical models.

These ethical frameworks provide the bedrock from which our principles and codes of conduct are drawn. While numerous ethical frameworks exist, our focus will be on three specific ones that form the foundation of many derivative theories. These are virtue ethics, consequentialism, and the theory of duty.

These theories, collectively referred to as normative theories, serve as guides for determining what actions are morally permissible or impermissible within various contexts, personal, societal, and professional, and how we ought to behave under different circumstances.

Normative theories provide frameworks for determining moral principles and evaluating ethical dilemmas and act as a guide to help us apply these in specific situations. For example, what applies to business ethics differs from what applies to engineering ethics, bioethics, environmental ethics, and so on.

While normative ethical theories are concerned with how we should broadly analyze actions to determine how we ought to behave, in applied ethics, we utilize these normative theories to align them with established normative principles.

Applied ethics involves the practical application of ethical principles to real-world scenarios, aiding individuals and organizations alike in making morally sound decisions. In the realm of business ethics, for example, these theories can help assess the ethical implications of practices such as fair labor practices, work-life balance, or corporate social responsibility programs.

To provide a concrete example of how normative theories and applied ethics work together without delving into excessive detail, consider a theory stipulating that we have a duty to avoid causing harm. This normative principle guides our behavior. However, its application varies across contexts.

In medicine, it means doctors should not voluntarily harm patients. A similar expectation applies to engineers, businesses, and so forth in their duty toward their customers and users. Yet, the types of harm each profession might cause differ significantly. That's why different ethical committees convene to explore what harm means within their profession and what necessary practices should be implemented to prevent it.

My focus in the coming chapters will mainly be on normative frameworks, with only an occasional example of applied ethics here and there.

In the previous part of this book, we concluded our discussion by emphasizing the significance of moral responsibility in the choices we make. This is because, despite our complete freedom to determine how we want to live and the meaning of our lives, we do not exist in isolation. Our decisions carry consequences that impact not only us but also others, both directly and indirectly.

Now, let's explore the frameworks that aid us in examining our conduct and determining what is morally right. These principles guide us in contributing to the common good, whether within our family, society, company, business, or country. To begin, let's delve into virtue ethics, developed by the ancient Greek philosopher Aristotle.

Chapter 8: Virtue Ethics

What kind of person do you want to be? What character traits and habits would you like to cultivate? Would you like to be an honest person? Perhaps a bit more courageous to say it as it is? What about physical and mental fitness? Is cultivating healthy habits something you aspire to and include in your yearly resolutions?

Let's sprinkle some humility and temperance (self-restraint) in there. Maybe this will make you more approachable, and you'll be able to foster more friendships. But what about conflicts and moral dilemmas? How do you plan to address these challenges? The most effective strategy for handling these situations often involves prioritizing fairness and justice in your decision-making. Did we overlook anything? We can consider infusing some humor and a touch of generosity to enrich our approach. What other elements could we explore?

I wouldn't be exaggerating if I assert that we all theoretically aspire to cultivate these character traits. Ideally, we want to be wise, fair, just, temperate, honest, humble, generous, and fit.

Imagine if we were able to establish a society, a community, or a business where people actively pursue and develop these habits. What would this society look like? This society or community would act harmoniously and collaboratively to solve problems, eradicate disease and poverty, contribute to the common good, and ensure that everyone is living a happy and content life.

Practically, this vision is easier said than done. Imagination is a free activity, though! Despite it being a utopian scenario that may be easier to implement in small communities than on a larger scale, it does, however, provide us with a good idea of the basic tenets of virtue theory.

In a nutshell, virtue theory, which was a staple framework in ancient Greece but was formalized and laid out by the ancient Greek philosopher Aristotle (384 — 322 BCE), views ethics as a set of laudable character traits referred to as virtues that we ought to pursue, develop, cultivate, and pass on in order to live a good and virtuous life and build just, collaborative, harmonious, and ethical or virtuous societies that care for the common good.

The premise is that if people become habituated to these virtues, then it will, by and large, be guaranteed that vice or bad behavior will be generally curbed.

One way of looking at it is through the prism of 'give a man a fish, and you feed him for a day; teach a man how to fish, and you'll feed him forever.' Instead of teaching people what is ethical or not in varying contexts, professions, and scenarios, a better approach, according to virtue theory, is to help build a virtuous character. Just like learning how to fish, by habituating ourselves to virtuous actions, our conduct and decision-making would align with the best ethical decision depending on the context.

At face value, this framework seems fairly easy and straightforward. All we have to do is determine praiseworthy values and think of a way to get everyone to pursue them. Not so simple, is it?

Chances are you've come across several articles that stress the importance of ethical leadership, for example. Could you, based on the aforementioned, think of what this might mean from a virtue framework? What are some important character traits, or virtues that leaders ought to cultivate to qualify for the label 'ethical leaders'?

Really, what does a good leader look like? We'll get back to this in more detail by examining Aristotle's account of virtue ethics. First, let's discuss the weatherman Phil Connors' tragicomic story.

Groundhog Day

Phil Connors is a narcissist and self-centered man. He doesn't really care much about other people and does not shy away from treating them with disdain and contempt. His actions are driven by egotistical desires mixed with self-aggrandizement. He refers to himself as 'the talent'. So much so, he barely does his job as a weatherman, and to the extent possible avoids any job-related tasks that don't really pique his interest.

But all of that is going to change on a cold February morning when he realizes that he is stuck in a time loop, waking up to the same radio tune on the second of February, repeating the same day ad infinitum.

It all begins when Phil is sent to the small town of Punxsutawney in Pennsylvania alongside his producer Rita and cameraman Larry, to cover the Groundhog Day festivities on February second.

Phil does not mask his scorn for the people of this town and for these 'outdated' festivities. The highlight of these celebrations revolves around a groundhog, Punxsutawney Phil. The entire town gathers to witness Phil come out of his burrow to predict whether there will be six more weeks of winter if Phil does see his shadow, or an early spring if he doesn't see his shadow.

Groundhog Day festivities and Punxsutawney Phil are factual. But the weatherman Phil getting stuck in an endless time loop is the plot of the movie Groundhog Day (1993) directed by Harold Ramis. The main character, Phil, is played by Bill Murray.

At first, Phil is discombobulated by the realization that he is stuck in a time loop akin to Sisyphus pushing the boulder uphill only for it to fall back again, and so on. He first shares this problem with Rita, the producer, who prompts him to see a doctor and a psychiatrist, to no avail.

The problem persists, but Phil gradually notices that his actions have no consequence whatsoever. So he starts living 'carpe diem' without any reservations, engaging in all sorts of activities, including theft, police chases, and other misdemeanors.

Phil eventually becomes bored, repeating the same day time and again. Even his attempts at suicide don't break him out of the loop. Eventually, he embarks on a transformative journey, and his attitude and character begin to change.

Slowly, he begins to care for and help other people. He starts doing his job with more enthusiasm and dedication. In addition, he takes up piano lessons and begins learning French, indulging in activities he genuinely enjoys. He invests more time cultivating good relationships with those he encounters and deepens his bonds with his colleagues, Larry and Rita. He even starts dating Rita and develops a strong affection for her.

Phil steadily pursues more meaning in his life, develops good habits, becomes more virtuous, and finds purpose in the activities he undertakes. This loop continues until one day he wakes up next to Rita with whom he spends the night. Phil realizes that his transformation, his pursuit of a meaningful and virtuous life, broke the cycle that had once trapped him.

Through a process of repetition, tinkering, and iteration, Phil develops good habits that help him improve his life and make him an overall better, moral, professional, and reliable person. After all, habits cannot be acquired overnight; they require constant practice, refinement, and habituation. This process is similar to fishing. You don't become a fisherman by trying it once; you become a skilled fisher when you've learned the ropes, made the practice a habit, and constantly improved your technique until you achieve excellence.

The Framework

It is this model that the virtue theory framework aims to implement.

Virtue theory proclaims that we ought to incorporate certain virtues, defined as excellent traits, as part of our characters by habituating ourselves to the practice of such traits as honesty, courage, etc. The opposite of virtue is vice.

Proponents of the theory, including Aristotle, suggest that, ideally, we ought to do what is virtuous and refrain from acting viciously. The assumption is that cultivating a good character is conducive to a society that functions in an orderly, harmonious, and cohesive manner. This is made possible insofar as a community acts virtuously with a view toward achieving the greater 'common' good, as we've already discussed.

What does all that mean? Why is it important to try to think about virtues to pursue individually and collectively? Are those universal? How do we decide which traits to cultivate?

For Aristotle, the good of the city is more important than the good of the individual. He argues that political leaders should be tasked with finding a suitable set of virtues that a community ought to revere and practice. Given their role as governors, politicians should work for the greater good; this includes deciding on and promoting certain virtues that would contribute to that end.

Of course, this might be counterintuitive nowadays because, in many instances, politicians to a large extent end up doing what is in their best interest. This was not always the case in ancient Greece.

It is important to keep in mind that Aristotle isn't interested in deriving, defining, or determining virtues and vices. Rather, he's going to base his arguments on cardinal virtues (wisdom, courage, temperance, and justice) that were commonly accepted by the ancient Greeks, as we've seen in the chapter on Stoicism, and he will proceed to explain how we can acquire them.

It is most likely that the surviving Aristotle's writings are lecture notes intended for his students at the Lyceum, which was the name of the academy he founded.

Aristotle sets out to develop his ethical framework in a treatise called *Nicomachean Ethics* (probably named after his son Nicomachus who edited it), showing how members of a society can live a good and practical life.

Happiness, the Chief Good, and Excellence

In the following passages, I will explain the concept of Eudaimonia, which roughly translates to happiness, flourishing, and contentment. Then I'll turn to an examination of Arete (virtue and excellence), as well as the character traits that would make this possible.

The first question Aristotle is going to ask is as follows: what do human beings seek in life? Every action or inquiry that we undertake seems to be seeking some sort of good, either as a means to an end or as an end in itself. We seek instrumental goods as a means to an end because what we ultimately care for is the chief good, which is happiness.

For example, we seek education to find a job, to make a living, to live decently... to be happy.

What does it mean to be happy? Aristotle explains that there are different conceptions of it. Some people associate it with honor, others with pleasure, and some with wealth. Some even attempt to define it abstractly and end up associating it with the intellect.

Aristotle considers material 'possessions' a possible source of happiness but argues that because of their ephemeral nature, we can't depend on them to reach a state of contentment and tranquility. It is essential, as a result, to examine human nature more deeply to find out which 'good' could potentially be the source of long-lasting 'Eudaimonia.' This chief good, as Aristotle calls it, can be pursued (and perhaps acquired) by living in accordance with what distinguishes us, as humans, from other species: reason. Here's how Aristotle defends his stance.

In order to determine the definition of the good, we need to figure out the function of the subject in question. A doctor's function is to heal or treat people; a carpenter's is to build good furniture; running shoes, to be durable. A good doctor, therefore, is someone who fulfills her function.

Aristotle asserts that there is no universal definition of the substance of goodness. Instead, goodness has different qualities that are relative to us. For instance, the goodness of a doctor, a carpenter, an athlete, and a human being may differ.

Aristotle divides the good into three different kinds:

1. Of the body (physical: health, food, drink).
2. External (honor, wealth, status).
3. Of the soul (intellect, virtues, knowledge).

What is the function of human beings? To determine this, we need to examine the function of all animate beings in nature, including plants, animals, and humans.

All three of them require nutrients for survival; animals and humans are both conscious in a way that plants might not be. Humans are distinct from both animals and plants in that we are rational animals, according to Aristotle.

Because we are rational, it follows that our function as human beings is to act rationally; i.e., to live in accordance with reason.

Aristotle links the good of something to its underlying function. We still need to figure out what would constitute good character traits and what constitutes living in accordance with reason.

According to Aristotle, virtues lie in the middle between two extremes: excesses and deficiencies. Living in accordance with reason means adopting a balanced approach. It's the continuous pursuit of the mean between these two extremes.

Our function, to live in accordance with reason, would be fulfilled when we seek the mean and incorporate it into our mode of action. Since this is an ongoing quest that concerns itself with acquiring excellent traits and honing our character, we need to cultivate the habit of pursuing moderation. This equally applies to our feelings and actions. The goal is to determine the appropriate kind of feeling or to act moderately depending on the situation.

For Aristotle, virtues are common to society, and they are 'universal' insofar as they apply to the entire community, but acquiring them is relative, conditioned on the situation, the individual, and other factors. A moderate diet for an athlete is much different from that of a non-athlete.

While many moderate actions fall in between two extremes, for example, courage is the middle ground between foolhardiness and cowardice, some extremes don't have a middle ground, like murder, which is defined as taking an innocent life against its will (and not in self-defense or in battle) and is automatically considered a vice that has no mean.

When it is hard to determine where the mean lies on the spectrum of actions, all we need to do is go in the opposite direction of whatever our appetites desire. As such, if I naturally desire to sit down and do nothing all day long every day, doing things in moderation would mean going against my desire in the opposite direction until I find a middle ground between 'workaholism' and being a couch potato.

Intellectual vs. Practical Virtues

Aristotle distinguishes between practical and intellectual virtues.

1. Practical virtues: habituating ourselves to do what is virtuous.
2. Intellectual virtues: seeking theoretical knowledge.

As such, while knowledge is important, it is not sufficient. Their relationship is reciprocal. We need to engage in both to approximate ourselves to the acquisition of virtue. Being virtuous means habituating ourselves to seek the mean and to become disposed to always do the 'right' thing. Ultimately, a life of intellectual contemplation, coupled with practical virtues, would put one on the right path to becoming a magnanimous person, as seen in the transformative journey of Phil from Groundhog Day.

To sum up, the main focus of virtue ethics is on cultivating a good character to enable us to live a good, tranquil, and content life. As we become more virtuous individuals, we also transform into good citizens who care about the well-being of our community. As a result, we can strive to strike a balance between the individual, family, community, and society, seeking personal excellence while also contributing to the betterment and overall well-being of society.

Of course, this scenario might seem too idealistic to be immediately applicable. The virtue theory framework may not effortlessly transition into the complexities of the real world. The problem it addresses is indeed intricate and may not be obvious.

This ongoing challenge, still relevant today, can be summarized as follows: to some degree, sharing theoretical, technical, intellectual, and even practical knowledge across various fields and domains is relatively straightforward.

That's why we have well-established institutions, systems, and mechanisms to train people in all kinds of specialties like engineering, medicine, computer science, psychology, anthropology, carpentry, plumbing, teaching, etc.

The knowledge and experience people learn in these fields can be acquired, applied, and transferred to other domains as well. We can also determine how good or virtuous people are in their trades. The task is easier to accomplish in this case because of the nature of the knowledge, namely, what Aristotle calls intellectual and productive virtues. In other words, the nature of knowledge that underlies these activities is such that we can abstract it, teach it, learn it, and transfer it.

But when it comes to how we ought to conduct ourselves as social individuals, the situation is murkier and more difficult to handle. To behave and live well is not an easily acquired know-how. That's because it's extremely difficult to define and teach concepts like justice, wisdom, temperance, courage, and all the other virtues. Why? Because they are practical virtues that are extremely difficult to pin down or even teach.

Courage, for instance, is an elusive and fluid concept. It is also not a trait that you can develop by simply knowing its definition or by seeing examples of it. It relies more on a form of mimicking and continuous practice and refinement. It also manifests in different forms depending on the context. If you're a firefighter, being courageous while on duty means something completely different than if you are with your family displaying fortitude as a parent or navigating through treacherous terrain as a hiker with your friends.

The Virtuous Leader: Navigating the Dichotomy of Leadership

Now let's apply this more concretely to the case of leadership. What are some of the traits that make a good leader? I'll give you a moment to think of three of the most essential virtues a leader should have and cultivate.

The responses I gathered during the interviews I conducted varied significantly. The most common virtues mentioned were humility, empathy, and honesty. Other responses included transparency, understanding, fairness, patience, and creativity.

I think we can all agree that the aforementioned virtues make up not only good leaders but good individuals too. However, the question remains: How can one genuinely develop into a competent leader or professional? As previously discussed, Aristotle's virtue theory framework suggests that we should reflect on these virtues, strive for a balanced approach between extremes, and seek excellence by instilling these virtues through habitual practice and practical application.

A more contemporary approach, echoing this Aristotelian framework, is presented by authors and retired Navy SEALs officers Jocko Willink and Leif Babin in their book titled "The Dichotomy of Leadership." When I initially encountered this book, I immediately recognized its application of Aristotle's principles in a business context. The book, while not explicitly mentioning Aristotle, mirrors the virtue theory framework and addresses the enduring problem that philosophers have grappled with for ages.

The key concept in their approach is the term 'dichotomy.' Willink and Babin explain that to become a skilled leader, one must learn to navigate endless dichotomies characterized by opposing forces on each side. They assert that a good leader must "carefully balance between these opposite forces." Among these opposing forces, none are as challenging as the need to deeply care for each team member while simultaneously accepting the risks necessary to achieve a mission. A good leader builds powerful, strong relationships with subordinates, but they must also recognize that there is a job to be done, a job that may put the very people they care deeply about at risk.

Throughout the book, they address various dichotomies drawing from their experiences in Iraq, extracting principles that can be readily applied in a business setting. Here are a few examples of the dichotomies that a leader ought to balance, as Willink and Babin suggest:

1. *They must be resolute but not overbearing.*
2. *They must know when to mentor and when to fire.*
3. *Be disciplined, but not rigid.*
4. *Be a leader, and a follower.*
5. *Be humble, but not passive.*

6. *They must plan, but not overplan.*

As Willink puts it, to avoid being either overbearing or too resolute, a leader must "correctly balance these two leadership styles, finding the middle ground, and paying attention to the team to ensure they don't push too far in one direction or the other. Clear warning signs indicate when a leader has leaned too far toward one of these leadership styles."

This approach closely aligns with Aristotelian philosophy. Willink and Babin authored "The Dichotomy of Leadership" in response to the challenges faced by business leaders who had previously read their other book, "Extreme Ownership."

These leaders encountered difficulties when applying the four laws of combat outlined in "Extreme Ownership," which include: 1) cover and move, 2) simple over complex, 3) prioritize and execute, and 4) decentralized command.

While diligently following these principles and embracing extreme ownership of their decisions, leaders often found themselves trapped in extremes, either oversimplifying or excessively prioritizing. This prompted Willink and Babin to write "The Dichotomy of Leadership" to emphasize that excellence resides in the middle ground between extremes, echoing Aristotle's perspective.

Running a business, managing clients, leading a team, and extracting the best from people necessitate more than just technical skills and knowledge. It demands a profound understanding of what it takes to become a virtuous person and a conscious effort to cultivate these traits. This journey requires internal and external self-awareness, introspection, and an unwavering commitment to self-improvement.

It also entails the willingness to be vulnerable, make mistakes, and accept feedback to develop these habits, as we previously explored in the earlier section.

So, the next time you find yourself caught between two opposing forces, consider it from the standpoint of virtue ethics. What underlying trait does the situation demand? Where does the middle ground lie? And how will you implement your decision? Ultimately, as Willink aptly puts it:

"Every leader must walk a fine line... Leadership necessitates finding equilibrium amid the dichotomy of seemingly contradictory qualities, between one extreme and another. Recognizing this balance is one of the most potent tools a leader possesses. With this in mind, a leader can more effectively harmonize opposing forces and lead with maximum effectiveness."

Chapter 9: Consequentialism

Lieutenant Commander Ronald Hunter, the Executive Officer of the Submarine Alabama, faces a difficult yet crucial decision in a split second. These few seconds feel like an eternity as he attempts to balance the potential outcomes of the available decision tree.

The choices are not complicated on the surface; he must either order the sealing of the bilge bay or wait a few more seconds to do so. However, therein lies the problem: the bilge bay is flooding with three sailors trapped inside. The bilge bay, a compartment at the bottom of the submarine designed to manage and contain water, has become a critical focal point of this life-and-death decision.

As time passes, the rescue of the trapped sailors becomes increasingly challenging. If the bilge bay is not sealed, the submarine will continue to sink and eventually implode, resulting in the loss of everyone onboard. If it is sealed, the three sailors will die, but control over the submarine will be regained.

The Chief of the Boat recommends immediately shutting the bilge bay. Hunter asks if the crew can rescue the sailors. The response is negative, so he gives the order to seal the compartment.

Before we proceed, put yourself in Hunter's shoes. What would you have done?

This example is quite extreme, as you've noted. It's a fictional scene from the movie "Crimson Tide," directed by Tony Scott and starring Gene Hackman and Denzel Washington. The movie is inspired by a real incident that occurred during the Cuban missile crisis.

Even though this is a fictional and extreme scenario, similar situations are occasionally faced by army generals, doctors, politicians, and professionals in real life. I believe it serves as a good entry point into the consequentialist ethics framework.

The dilemma that Hunter faced required him to make an immediate decision, and any action he took would have resulted in death. Can we judge any of these decisions as morally right or wrong? What do you think?

The consequentialist ethics framework stipulates that there are no inherently right or wrong actions. We cannot assess an action or a decision and definitively label it as morally right or wrong. According to this framework, actions are value-neutral, and from this point onward, I will adhere to the consequentialist perspective unless specified otherwise.

What we need to examine are the consequences of the action, conducting a balance of the pros and cons while measuring the degrees of harm and benefits that the decision or action leads to.

In Hunter's case, the order he gave to seal the bilge bay cannot be analyzed in isolation. If you scrutinize his decision, you may argue that it's unethical because he left three men behind to face their deaths. This assessment holds if you were evaluating the action itself.

However, when considering the consequences of the action, various factors come into play to determine which course of action or decision is morally appropriate, or perhaps, more morally adequate in this particular case.

Main Principles of Consequentialist Ethics

The consequentialist framework, as we've seen from the previous example, focuses on the outcomes of actions rather than the actions themselves. The central argument of consequentialism is that an action is considered moral if, on balance, its consequences result in more good than harm, making it overall good.

Consequently, we should consistently and persistently choose actions that ultimately lead to more good than harm. This is a fantastic and commendable goal. I think we all condone this. However, the crucial question is: What kind of good are we striving to maximize? What will be the assessment criteria or guiding principles to determine whether the consequences truly maximize the good while minimizing negative outcomes?

The consequentialist framework serves as a broad foundation for numerous subsequent theories that derive from it. These theories include, among many others:

- **Utilitarianism,** which argues that we should maximize the greatest good, happiness, and utility for the greatest number of people.

- **Egoism**, which posits that we should pursue our self-interests and maximize our own well-being.
- **Altruism**, which suggests that we should maximize the well-being of others, sometimes at our own expense. **Effective altruism** stems from this perspective, with its main argument being that the best way to maximize the well-being of others is by choosing the best and most effective actions, supported by empirical evidence. If you are not familiar with effective altruism, I encourage you to look up SBF, the FTX guy, to learn more about how it could go wrong.

In what follows, I will only focus on the utilitarian framework because, by and large, I would venture to say that it's the most common and well-known consequentialist theory. As previously mentioned, my goal isn't to critique these theories or argue for or against them. Instead, my goal is to provide you with enough foundation to understand the theoretical basis of some major ethical frameworks and equip you with the tools needed to identify the underlying principles and frameworks used in various arguments and to conduct an ethical analysis yourself.

Utilitarianism

Utilitarianism has been one of the most influential normative ethical theories. It was formally developed by English philosopher and jurist Jeremy Bentham (1748 — 1832). However, its precursors can be found in the writings of philosophers like Francis Hutcheson (1694 — 1746) and David Hume (1711 — 1776). The seed of utilitarianism can be traced all the way back to the ancient Greek philosopher Epicurus (341 — 270 BCE), who developed the philosophical school of thought known as Epicureanism.

A brief tangent: the Epicureans were the direct rivals of the Stoics, whom we discussed in the second part of this book.

Utilitarianism, in a nutshell, is premised on the principle that an action is moral if it brings happiness, utility, and well-being to the greatest number of people. For utilitarians, the good is identified with actions that bring us pleasure in the long run, and the bad is associated with actions that cause pain in the long run.

This principle is known as the hedonic principle, which stipulates that we ought to pursue what brings us long-term pleasure and happiness and avoid what will cause us long-term harm and pain.

Two simple examples to convey this point before delving deeper are as follows: exercising is good for us because, despite the short-term pain we endure, it ultimately brings us happiness and well-being. We should avoid consuming drugs because, while pleasure-inducing in the short term, the overall consequences are bad and harmful in the long run.

The hedonic principle was originally posited and developed by Epicurus and the Epicureans, for whom "pleasure is the goal that nature has ordained for us; it is also the standard by which we judge everything good."

However, as we saw in the exercising example, the hedonic principle was not meant to encourage us to pursue an unhinged life, seeking pleasure at all costs. According to the Epicureans, we attain pleasure when we satisfy our basic natural and necessary needs, such as food and water, shelter, and physical fitness.

The Epicureans divided pleasures into three categories:

- Natural and necessary: food, shelter, fitness
- Natural but unnecessary: luxury food and shelter
- Unnatural and unnecessary: wealth, status, power

To live a good, pleasurable, happy, and tranquil life devoid of avoidable physical and mental pain and suffering, we should only strive to fulfill our natural and necessary needs, according to Epicurus. They were the original minimalists who aimed to declutter their lives and focus only on what was necessary.

Counter-intuitive as that may be, the idea is that by indulging and seeking to actively satisfy our desire for power, status, and wealth, we bring upon ourselves a great deal of anxiety and unnecessary pain. In contrast, by focusing on what really matters, we would not only be attaining pleasure but also eradicating avoidable pain and suffering along the way. Avoidable, I stress, because some injuries, disease, and other pains may be inevitable. What matters are the long-term results, and not the short-term bouts of pleasure.

It is important to keep this in mind because this hedonic principle would inspire several 18th-century philosophers such as Francis Hutcheson and David Hume, whose moral philosophies would be foundational in the development of utilitarianism.

For Hutcheson, for instance, the hedonic principle is formulated such that **'the action is best which produces the greatest happiness for the greatest numbers.'** Hume uses the term 'utility' to refer to the sense of satisfaction that people derive from their actions.

Hume's friend, philosopher Adam Smith, among others, incorporates the term utility in his economic analysis. But I digress.

Jeremy Bentham's Hedonic Calculus

Jeremy Bentham picked up these two principles, the hedonic principle and the maximization of well-being for the greatest number of people, and proceeded to develop the basics of utilitarianism. If we want to ensure that individuals, communities, societies, and countries function well, our actions, decisions, and policies should aim to maximize their overall well-being.

On an individual level, this means enabling people to pursue what brings them pleasure and happiness, insofar as it does not infringe on the well-being of, or harm, others. On a societal level, it means establishing norms and policies that would help individuals and groups alike actualize and develop themselves, and that would aim to curb the problems that cause suffering and pain, including disease and poverty.

The main objective is clear and simple. Individually and collectively, we are better off pursuing that which brings happiness to the greatest number of people or, at the very least, does not inflict harm on others.

For example, according to utilitarians, murder, or the unlawful premeditated killing of someone against their will, is considered wrong not because there's something inherently bad with murder itself, but rather because the overall consequences of murder lean towards causing more harm than promoting positive well-being.

This assessment takes into account the psychological and physical harm inflicted on the victim's loss of life, their family, and friends, as well as the broader negative consequences associated with normalizing such actions and the catastrophic results that could ensue if everyone were allowed to engage in it.

Ideally, therefore, we want to eradicate poverty, disease, and any related issues that may cause suffering, and we want to promote that which helps everyone live well. But we also need to keep in mind that we aim for long-term solutions. As mentioned earlier, it is not short-term pleasures or pains that utilitarians strive for or avoid, but rather that which evokes long-term well-being.

The problem Bentham faced revolved around identifying the sources of pleasure or pain, evaluating, and measuring them. He was aware that individuals derive pleasure from a range of differing interests and actions. So establishing some sort of objective criteria to evaluate and optimize the pleasures and pains associated with different interests, decisions, and actions proved to be a complex task.

This problem would later vex economists too. When I say that I derive pleasure from eating a burger, what does that exactly mean? It is quite difficult to quantify and qualify such an experience.

The amount of pleasure I derive from eating a burger may not be the same as yours, and the best proof of all this is the diminishing marginal utility. That is, the fact that the more we consume something, the less pleasure we derive from it. Maybe I derive pleasure from binge-watching 10 episodes of a Netflix series, whereas by the 5th episode of the same series, you may feel like you've had enough for the day.

But I digress, again. Bentham wanted to devise a clear method or framework that made the evaluation of pleasure and pain as objective and as quantifiable as possible. This, he thought, would help individuals and societies maximize their well-being in a rational and objective manner.

To facilitate the establishment of common ground and a unified system for determining and articulating sensations of pleasure or pain, Jeremy Bentham developed the hedonic calculus. This method allows for the measurement of the pains and pleasures associated with a specific action or decision.

Bentham's hedonic calculus includes several criteria. For each criterion, a certain value is assigned to the potential pain and pleasure associated with it. Then the overall values of pleasure and pain are summed up respectively and compared. If the balance is positive, then the action is ethical; otherwise, it would be wrong to pursue it.

- **Intensity:** how powerful the action is.
- **Duration:** how long it lasts.
- **Certainty or uncertainty:** how certain or uncertain the outcomes or consequences are.
- **Remoteness**: how soon the outcomes will occur.
- **Richness**: the extent of pleasures it will lead to.
- **Purity**: if it is free of pain or not.
- **Extent**: how many people will be affected by it.

Let's take exercise as a simple example. Say the values range from 1 to 5, with 1 being the lowest and 5 being the highest.

Aspect: Intensity

- Pleasure (e.g., endorphin release, improved mood): 4

- Pain (e.g., physical exertion, soreness): -3

Aspect: Duration

- Pleasure (Medium-term - during and immediately after exercise): 3
- Pain (Short-term - during exercise and recovery): -2

Aspect: Certainty or uncertainty

- Pleasure (Highly certain): 3
- Pain (Highly certain): -3

Aspect: Remoteness

- Pleasure (Immediate mood improvement after exercise): 4
- Pain (Immediate physical exertion during exercise): -4

Aspect: Richness

- Pleasure (Potential for long-term health benefits and increased energy): 5
- Pain (Potential for occasional injuries or discomfort): -2

Aspect: Purity

- Pleasure (Predominantly pleasure with some discomfort): 3
- Pain (Predominantly discomfort with occasional positive feelings): -2

Aspect: Extent

- Pleasure (Benefits the individual primarily): 4
- Pain (Only the individual experiences discomfort): -4

Total pleasure: 26 | Total pain: -20

Given the above, it appears that exercise leads to happiness and well-being, and therefore, it is preferable to pursue it over not exercising. This is just a simple example that would be used in more complicated analyses to determine whether to build a highway, a park, a hospital, a school, etc. The hedonic calculus, Bentham thought, would help us make more effective and better decisions that would be conducive to happiness and well-being on individual as well as collective levels.

John Stuart Mill's Higher Pleasures

Enter philosopher and political economist John Stuart Mill (1806 — 1873). Mill was Bentham's student. Although he absorbed and advocated utilitarianism as an ethical framework, he was not really happy with Bentham's approach. He even indirectly called it akin to pig philosophy. This may have probably earned him a block on social media or something.

Mill's approach to utilitarianism and his main criticism of Bentham's methodology could be summed up in this Mill quote: "It is better to be a human being dissatisfied than a pig satisfied; better to be Socrates dissatisfied than a fool satisfied."

Mill did not particularly like that Bentham treated all pleasures as equal in value. For Bentham, there was no difference in the quality or value of pleasure derived from reading a book, traveling, exercising, having a thoughtful conversation with people, taking long walks in a park, attending a party, listening to music, being healthy, being wealthy, having sex, or eating a hamburger. Bentham did not distinguish between pleasures or between the quantity and quality that people derived from their actions.

Mill thought this was problematic because the hedonic calculus, as developed by Bentham, promoted all pleasures as equal, and it made it possible for people to infringe on the rights of others because everyone would be seeking pleasures at all costs, particularly physical pleasures. That's why he thought that Bentham's philosophy promoted physical pleasures more so than any other kind of pleasures that may be qualitatively better.

Instead, Mill maintained Bentham's calculus but acknowledged that some pleasures are qualitatively better than others.

Mill thought that we would be better off and happier if we pursued what he called higher pleasures and not only focused on the lower pleasures. For him, higher pleasures included intellectual, moral, and emotional pleasures that we derive from engaging in literature, art, philosophy, and music, and from the satisfaction we get from acts of kindness, fairness, honesty, and temperance.

According to Mill, these higher pleasures are more worthy of pursuit than the lower, physical, and bodily pleasures like enjoying food, beverages, sex, and comfort. The gratification derived from higher pleasures is more intense and longer-lasting than that from lower ones.

Consequently, when faced with a decision between building, for example, a park or a public library versus an entertainment center, Mill would argue that the morally correct decision would be to choose the park or public library because it promotes higher pleasures.

In a particular society, the challenge is therefore to find a balance between lower and higher pleasures, all the while ensuring that individuals are free to pursue their interests insofar as they do not harm others. This delicate balance is ideally established by ensuring that the government protects the liberties of individuals and promotes their well-being, combats disease and poverty, and encourages activities that make it easier for people to indulge in the higher pleasures in addition to the lower ones.

Applied in a business context, this means that the leaders within any enterprise ought to ensure the well-being of their employees. They should make decisions, take action, and create a workspace that contributes to their happiness and overall well-being. In other words, business leaders should prioritize not only the financial success of the company and the well-being of the employees but also the cultivation of a workplace culture that encourages the pursuit of higher pleasures. This approach aligns with Mill's utilitarian philosophy, promoting a more fulfilling and morally sound work environment.

Hume, Bentham, and Mill, among others, played a crucial role in the development and consolidation of utilitarianism, which, as we saw, is one derivative of the consequentialist framework. There are also several kinds of utilitarianism, including act utilitarianism (which evaluates individual actions separately) and rule utilitarianism (which focuses on a set of rules that aim to maximize well-being), but I won't bore you with that here.

The point of this part and this chapter is simply to give you an overview of the underlying dynamics of ethical analysis, moral reasoning, and decision-making.

Utilitarianism aims to maximize the greatest good for the greatest number of people. The main utilitarian principle is that seeking long-term pleasure and avoiding preventable pain is good. To maximize overall utility, happiness, and well-being, we ought to pursue actions that, on balance, gratify us more than they cause pain.

As a result, actions are neither inherently right nor wrong but are judged based on their consequences. This is the main guiding principle for utilitarians in deciding between ethical dilemmas such as misleading marketing, laying off employees in times of crisis, building highways or parks, and deciding on bioethical, environmental, or financial matters.

So to go back to the Crimson Tide example, how would you analyze Hunter's decision to order the sealing of the bilge bay?

Here's another, more business-related case for you to consider.

"You're a manager in a company. You discover that a colleague, a single parent who is well-liked and has worked in the company for over a decade, is stealing office supplies regularly to sell and supplement their income. They are unaware that you've discovered their actions." From a utilitarian perspective, what would be the best action to undertake in this case?

In approaching the situation, think about all the possible actions at your disposal, then proceed to evaluate the pros and cons of each action. You may want to report your colleague, confront them privately, or offer to provide financial assistance.

If you decide to report your colleague, you may maintain your integrity as well as that of the company, but you may cause your colleague problems that affect their job security and well-being, including the well-being of their dependents.

If you decide to confront them privately, you may help them save face and convince them not to repeat their actions. On the downside, they may not heed your advice, and by not setting an example, others may not be deterred from carrying out the same actions.

If you decide to offer them financial assistance, you may address the root cause of the problem and help your colleague improve their financial situation. On the downside, it may be unfair to offer preferential treatment and keep the door open for others to resort to similar behavior.

There may also be alternative actions that you can choose from. But assuming that you only have these three options to choose from, and knowing that from a utilitarian perspective, you ought to choose the action that maximizes happiness and well-being for the greatest number of people, which of the three options above would you go for?

We have thus far explored two different ethical models. Virtue ethics focuses on developing good character by pursuing positive traits while refraining from vices. One example of virtue ethics is Aristotle's theory. In contrast to focusing on character, consequentialist frameworks assess the outcomes of actions to determine their moral alignment. utilitarianism, for example, falls under consequentialism.

In the following chapter, we will examine a third model known as the theory of duty or deontology. This broad framework assesses the morality of an action not by its consequences but by analyzing the action itself. Deontology assumes that actions are either inherently right or wrong and that we are well-equipped to evaluate their quality. By discerning the morality of an action, we consequently have a moral duty to either pursue it or refrain from doing it.

Some theories that fall under the umbrella of deontology include religious ethics, which posit that God and the scriptures serve as the source of moral judgment. Another theory, which will be our main focus, is Kant's moral philosophy. Kant believed that human beings can judge the morality of an action by using reason.

But first, let's meet Amadeu de Prado.

Chapter 10: Theory of Duty (Deontology)

Amadeu de Prado was a medical doctor who happened to live in Portugal during the Salazar dictatorship (1928 — 1974). De Prado was not only a good doctor who upheld his Hippocratic oath, treating his patients and abiding by the "do no harm" edict, but he was also popular and highly regarded by everyone in his neighborhood.

During that time, the Salazar regime had tight control over Portugal. Dissenting intellectual, cultural, and political voices were oppressed, curbed, and persecuted. An atmosphere of fear loomed over the Portuguese cities, including Lisbon, where Amadeu lived and worked. Kidnappings, persecutions, and tortures were carried out by the secret police, headed by José Mendes, nicknamed the "Butcher of Lisbon."

One ominous afternoon, de Prado's sister woke him up from his sacred half-hour nap, signaling an emergency. One that would thrust de Prado into the limelight and compel him to make a momentous professional decision that would haunt him for the rest of his life.

Lying on the table was the Butcher of Lisbon. He was severely injured, hovering between life and death with a stopped heart. De Prado had to make a choice: should he honor his duty as a doctor to save Mendes' life, or simply do nothing and let him die? Should he uphold his oath as a doctor to save patients' lives, or should he make a political choice, aiding the resistance and letting Mendes pass away?

Unflinchingly, de Prado decided to save Mendes' life. His duty as a doctor came first. Consequently, he was called a traitor by the people in his neighborhood, and the visits to his home clinic began to decline. Seeking atonement and redemption, he joined the clandestine resistance.

The decisive factor in this particular ethical dilemma was the duty that Amadeu de Prado had as a doctor toward patients, irrespective of who they were. Doctors are expected to do what's right, do no harm, and do their best to treat their patients. They are therefore bound to uphold actions that are considered morally right.

As a result, if saving a patient's life is intrinsically right as stipulated by medical ethics, then it is the doctor's duty to treat a patient irrespective of who they are or the consequences of the action, as in the case of utilitarianism.

Although Salazar is indeed a historical figure, the characters Mendes, Amadeu de Prado, and the Mendes incident constitute a fictional narrative. This story is featured in the novel "Night Train to Lisbon" by Peter Bieri, written under the pseudonym Pascal Mercier. However, such a dilemma is not far-fetched. Doctors and many other professionals face similar ethical dilemmas on a daily basis.

Fictional as it may be, this story serves as a good entry point into the theory of duty. In this framework, what matters are neither the virtues of the person nor the consequences of the action. What is essential is the action itself. The premise is that actions are either inherently right or intrinsically wrong. We, therefore, have a duty to pursue the actions that are moral and refrain from doing the actions that are immoral, irrespective of the consequences.

In other words, the theory of duty would argue that by saving Mendes' life, de Prado opted for the morally correct decision. Why? Because his duty as a doctor was to save lives. The concern is not whether his action would maximize the greater good for the greatest number of people, nor whether it would lead to more harm and destruction. The main focal point is on the action itself, and the ultimate goal is to stick to one's moral duty and do the right thing irrespective of one's intentions, desires, or will.

In a nutshell, according to the theory of duty, many actions possess intrinsic value. Upon examining the underlying actions and determining whether they are morally right or wrong, it becomes our duty to either carry them out or refrain from doing them.

The next logical step involves determining how we will analyze the actions to ascertain their morality or correctness.

As I've already mentioned, in religious ethics, God and the scriptures are the source of morality, and they serve as the ultimate authority to determine which actions are right and which are wrong. Within these parameters, there is some room for interpretation and speculation, but there is no debate about what is right or wrong.

One example would be the Ten Commandments, which are written in the form of 'thou shalt not.' They are orders, and religious people are bound by this covenant. They have a duty toward God.

I will not delve into religious ethics as it demands extensive contextualization and is a complex subject to tackle. Instead, in what follows I will concentrate on the moral theory proposed by German philosopher Immanuel Kant (1724 — 1804).

Kant's Categorical Imperative

Kant was born in a small city called Königsberg, Prussia (modern-day Kaliningrad, Russia). Kant never left his hometown. The farthest he got was only a few hundred kilometers on his commute to do private tutoring, which was his main source of income until he managed to secure a professorship at the University of Königsberg at the age of 46. Talk about perseverance and ambition! Kant never traveled and never displayed any curiosity for visiting or discovering other places.

He was happy where he lived and led a life bound by a highly regimented schedule down to the minute. So much so that it is said the people of Königsberg would set their clocks by his daily walks.

Kant would give morning lectures on various subjects, including history, geography, and philosophy. He would take walks, have one meal a day at lunch, usually accompanied by his friends and acquaintances, spend some time reading and writing, and go to bed early. He was a very sociable and likable guy.

Kant published numerous books during his lifetime and explored a wide range of topics. However, his most famous and seminal work is titled "Critique of Pure Reason," which he dedicated seven years to writing. The first edition of the book was so challenging for readers to understand that Kant had to revise and release a second edition.

The "Critique of Pure Reason" marks the beginning of a series of three critiques that build upon each other. The second critique, known as the "Critique of Practical Reason," is where Kant developed his ethical theory and framework. He expanded on his previous work, "Groundwork for the Metaphysics of Morals," which served as the foundation for his moral philosophy. The third critique is called the "Critique of Judgment," concerned with the nature of beauty, the sublime, and aesthetic taste.

In both the "Groundwork" and the second critique, Kant laid out the foundations for a theory of duty framework. Unlike religious ethics, for Kant, all human beings are equipped with the necessary rational faculties and tools to assess a particular action and determine its moral worth.

Because we are all equipped with the same rational tools, Kant argued that ethical reasoning ought to be absolute and universal. In other words, when examining an action from a rational standpoint and according to clear principles, the context would not matter because we would all arrive at the same conclusion. So whether you're in Lebanon or the United States, regardless of your cultural background, you would reach the same conclusion.

This is why Kant called the framework he proposed the "Categorical Imperative." "Categorical" because it's absolute and applies universally irrespective of the context or consequences, and "imperative" because we have a duty to do the right thing.

Kant's Categorical Imperative comprises several formulations, but I will only go over the first two. The goal of this exposition is to give you some insights into the reasoning process that lies behind this framework and not to make you an expert on Kant.

I would like to take a moment to crack a categorical imperative joke now, but I unfortunately Kant.

So before I go over the two formulations of the categorical imperative, let's go back to the example of Amadeu de Prado. Through this example, I will illustrate Kant's reasoning process and then proceed to provide the principles underlying the categorical imperative. This way, I believe, it would be easier to understand Kant's framework.

Kant would probably condone de Prado's decision to save Mendes. His rationale would be as follows: a doctor's purpose is to treat and cure patients and save lives to the extent possible. If doctors were to whimsically decide who should be treated and who shouldn't, then this would go against the very basic principle of being a doctor. Not to mention the arbitrariness and fickleness to which patients would be subjected, the majority of whom would want to be properly treated.

On the other hand, it would also be unfair to treat patients as means to a particular end, be it political or economic and financial benefits.

The relationship between a doctor and their patient should be governed by a sense of duty and should not be transactional. While a doctor may charge a fee for their services, taking advantage of and using the patients for purposes other than seeking to cure them would also be immoral.

Therefore, no matter who the patient is, a doctor is bound by their duty to attend to them. As a result, Kant's verdict would be that de Prado did the right thing.

This reasoning will serve as the foundation for Kant's categorical imperative in its two formulations.

The first focuses on whether the action contradicts a certain principle and whether it is universalizable. The second asserts that people should not, without their knowledge or consent, be taken advantage of or used as instruments for a particular goal, or as means to an end. This is because human beings have inherent moral worth and dignity, and they should be treated respectfully as ends in themselves. People's autonomy and dignity should be respected at all costs.

As such, Kant's theory of duty is based on the categorical imperative. The first two formulations are:

First formulation: Universality: "Act only according to that maxim whereby you can at the same time will that it should become a universal law."

Second formulation: Humanity: "Act in such a way that you treat humanity, whether in your own person or in the person of any other, never merely as a means to an end, but always at the same time as an end."

Here's another example to clarify these two formulations further. Let's assess whether keeping a promise is the moral thing to do or not. Say you made a promise to your friend that you will give them back the money you borrowed. However, you decide to break this promise for your convenience. Is this action morally right or wrong?

The first formulation examines whether the action is universalizable, assuming that everyone does the action and determining whether it would hold. In the case of breaking a promise, if everyone were to break their promises, then the concept of a promise becomes void and meaningless. As a result, breaking one's promise is immoral, and it is our duty to keep our promises, regardless of the conditions or context.

Similarly, for the second formulation, if breaking the promise is merely convenient for us, we would be treating our friend as a means to an end, using them to get their money. In this case, we would neither be respecting their autonomy nor their moral dignity. Therefore, it's immoral to break a promise, regardless of the circumstance.

I understand if you think Kant is a bit too much. His framework, the categorical imperative, and the broader theory of duty defend the premise that there has to be a way for us to determine whether an action is right or wrong independent of the situation.

The reason why Kant and the deontologists advocate this stance is that they fear that without a clear set of criteria to help us assess the moral quality of actions, we could easily fall into the trap of relativism, and it becomes extremely difficult to agree on a baseline.

Whether or not you are ready to embrace the Kantian framework is a decision you will have to make. Of course, I could spend a lot of time critiquing each of the theories I presented above, but this would make the book longer and more tedious to go through.

I reiterate that the main goal here is to provide you with a basic exposition of these major theories so that you gain insight into the ethical decision-making process adopted by various frameworks. So the next time you hear someone talking about one's duty to carry out a certain action, you will know the underlying assumptions of their stance. This will help you identify the reasons behind their argument, and you may be better equipped to push back, explore their argument further, and perhaps bridge the gap and establish common ground.

The DuPont Case Under the Kantian Prism

One real-life example of individuals going above and beyond the call of duty is the case of lawyer Robert Bilott in the lawsuit against DuPont's production of Teflon, which contained a carcinogenic and poisonous substance known as PFOA (perfluorooctanoic acid). Bilott, initially a corporate lawyer representing chemical firms, found his path redirected.

Two farmers from Parkersburg, West Virginia, reached out to him, imploring him to investigate their case. He initially refused but eventually agreed after witnessing the havoc caused by the chemical waste dumped by DuPont in the town.

The contamination, attributed later to PFOA, resulted in various physical and health problems. The land became arid, animals suffered deformities, and residents and DuPont factory workers developed cancers. Their teeth were disfigured, and their children began to show abnormalities.

After a lengthy legal battle, during which Bilott had risked his reputation and career, he succeeded in compelling DuPont to reach a settlement to provide compensation to those affected. He also shed light on the serious health issues associated with Teflon, prompting DuPont and the government to establish clear regulations to limit its usage.

From a theory of duty, especially a Kantian perspective, Bilott's actions were morally right. He fulfilled his duty to protect the citizens from the harm caused by the company. Conversely, DuPont failed in its duty as a company to ensure the safety of its customers, employees, and the local residents where the factory was situated.

According to the first formulation of the categorical imperative, allowing all corporations to prioritize profit at any cost would not be logically consistent. This is primarily because it contradicts the principles of health and environmental protection. Furthermore, this approach is likely to have adverse consequences as it leads to increasing harm, ultimately impacting businesses negatively.

According to the second formulation, DuPont's actions were morally wrong because they treated people merely as a means to an end, without respecting their autonomy, dignity, or mental and physical well-being. Consequently, by choosing to pursue this case, Bilott did the right thing.

So the next time you want to do the right thing, say choose to become a whistleblower in your company, take a look at Kant's ethics. It may sure be helpful!

Concluding remarks

I have gone through this entire part without mentioning "The Trolley Problem." That's quite an achievement if you ask me! But, oh well, I just did.

You may have come across this thought experiment before. Either way, it's usually popular in ethics courses because it sets the stage for what's to come. I decided to keep it until now because I want to leave you with some food for thought.

The trolley problem is a thought experiment aimed at exploring our responses to hypothetical ethical dilemmas. As we examine various scenarios within this thought experiment, layers of complexity are added to help us identify which moral theory framework we tend to use depending on the type of problem we are confronted with.

The trolley problem unfolds as follows: Picture yourself standing near a railroad track. You observe a trolley coming down the railway. Right beside you, there's a railway junction with a lever that can divert the trolley onto another track.

You notice that ahead of you five people are tied to one track, and the trolley is on a collision course with them. On the other track, there is one person who will die if you choose to pull the lever and change the trolley's course. So you face a choice: either allow five people to die by not pulling the lever, or take action by pulling the lever, resulting in the death of one person but saving five. What would you do in this situation?

One variation of the trolley problem is to imagine yourself standing on a bridge, and you have the choice to push an obese man onto the railway, thereby stopping the trolley from moving forward and saving all those tied on the track.

Another example that is usually given in this case is to imagine, instead, that you're a doctor, and you have the chance to kill one perfectly healthy person to use his organs to save five other patients who are hovering between life and death. For a compelling and fun in-depth examination of all these scenarios, you can check out Michael Sandel's "Justice: What's the Right Thing to Do" video available on YouTube[9]. It's a delight to listen to him facilitating the class discussion.

It's true that this is a thought experiment with preset and controlled variables. But the goal of this case is to get you to examine your reactions and probe the underlying assumptions and frameworks you inadvertently use when facing a moral dilemma.

More particularly, depending on whether you examine the consequences, the action, or the character of the person pulling the lever, pushing the obese guy, or the doctor killing or not the patients, you'd be able to notice whether you're using a consequentialist, a theory of duty, or a virtue ethics framework.

I won't be analyzing the trolley problem here, but I wanted to share it to get you to think about your reasoning process in each of the cases previously mentioned. What framework do you naturally lean toward? Can you challenge your belief and defend a different perspective, completely opposite to your own?

What if you found yourself in a situation similar to that of Doctor Amadeu de Prado, Lieutenant Commander Ronald Hunter, or Phil Connors from the examples previously mentioned? What do you think you would have done?

At the end of the day, to avoid falling into the Euthyphro trap, where Euthyphro believed the right thing to do was to directly prosecute his father, rather than following the ancient Greek law's requirement to

---

9   https://youtu.be/kBdfcR-8hEY

reach out to the victim's family, a more appropriate approach would be to adopt a Socratic perspective when facing a moral dilemma. Try to identify the underlying components of the issue you're facing and all the available details. Probe your assumptions. Examine things from different perspectives, and keep in mind that it is highly likely that the disagreements you have with others over the issue at hand may be due to the fact that you're addressing it using different ethical frameworks.

As Kant says:

> **"Two things fill the mind with ever new and increasing admiration and awe, the more often and steadily we reflect upon them: the starry heavens above me and the moral law within me."**

Conclusion

As the book comes to a close, I want to take this opportunity to thank you for taking the time to read through it. The process of writing is never easy, especially when deciding what to keep and what to leave out.

I still remember the first philosophy course I ever taught. I was so excited that I wanted to talk about everything I knew. As a result, I crammed the syllabus with so many readings that the reading packet was 300 pages long. Needless to say, the course was a flop.

Over time, I learned that it's better to keep things simple and to focus on a clear account that follows a particular storyline. This makes the material easier to remember and more compelling. I endeavored to follow a similar path while brainstorming and writing this book. There may be topics that I could have easily elaborated on or discussed in more detail. But my aim was to maintain, to the extent possible, an engaging narrative.

My main goal has been to present foundational philosophical concepts in a way that is relatable and actionable both in your personal and professional life. By exploring the importance of asking questions and questioning assumptions, navigating uncertainty and the quest for meaning, and examining ethical decision-making theories, I hope that I have been able to lay out a few frameworks and mental models that prove helpful for you as a professional or a business leader.

This book will be successful if it manages to get you to adopt a philosophical mindset and explore the topics discussed in these pages with your colleagues and friends. If you want to carry the conversation further, you can always reach out to me on social media (mainly X) @decafquest. Thank you!

Bibliography

This is a list of primary and secondary references. In this work, I have cited many of the books shown below. The others have directly and indirectly inspired many of the ideas present in it.

Aristotle. (2012). *Aristotle's Nicomachean Ethics* (R. C. Bartlett & S. D. Collins, Trans.; Reprint edition). University of Chicago Press.

Aurelius, M. (2006). *Meditations* (M. Hammond, Trans.). Penguin Classics.

Barrett, W. (1990). *Irrational Man: A Study in Existential Philosophy* (Reprinted edition). Anchor.

Bentham, J. (2017). *An Introduction to the Principles of Morals and Legislation*. CreateSpace Independent Publishing Platform.

Berger, W. (2016). *A more beautiful question: The power of inquiry to spark breakthrough ideas* (Paperback edition). Bloomsbury.

Bertrand, R. (2013). *The Problems of Philosophy*. Martino Fine Books.

Campbell, J. (2008). *The Hero with a Thousand Faces* (Third edition). New World Library.

Epstein, D. (2021). *Range: Why Generalists Triumph in a Specialized World*. Riverhead Books.

Eurich, T. (2018). *Insight: The Surprising Truth About How Others See Us, How We See Ourselves, and Why the Answers Matter More Than We Think* (Reprint edition). Currency.

Farnsworth, W. (2018). *The Practicing Stoic: A Philosophical User's Manual*. David R. Godine, Publisher.

Frankl, V. E., & Boyne, J. (2017). *Man's Search for Meaning: Young*

Adult Edition: Young Adult Edition (Reprint edition). Beacon Press.

Gregersen, H., & Catmull, E. (2018). *Questions Are the Answer: A Breakthrough Approach to Your Most Vexing Problems at Work and in Life.* Harper Business.

Hartley, S. (2017). *The fuzzy and the techie: Why the liberal arts will rule the digital world.* Houghton Mifflin Harcourt.

Herman, A. E. (2021). *Fixed.: How to Perfect the Fine Art of Problem Solving.* Harper.

Holiday, R. (2015). *Obstacle Is The Way* (Hand edition). Profile Books Ltd.

Horowitz, B. (2014). *The Hard Thing About Hard Things: Building a Business When There Are No Easy Answers.* Harper Business.

Hume, D. (1993). *An Enquiry Concerning Human Understanding: With Hume's Abstract of A Treatise of Human Nature and A Letter from a Gentleman to His Friend in Edinburgh* (E. Steinberg, Ed.; Second Edition,2). Hackett Publishing Company, Inc.

Hume, D., & Schneewind, J. B. (1983). *An Enquiry Concerning the Principles of Morals* (E. Steinberg, Ed.; Copyright 1983 edition). Hackett Publishing.

Iñiguez, S. (2022). *Philosophy Inc.: Applying Wisdom to Everyday Management* (1st ed. 2023 edition). Palgrave Macmillan.

Irvine, W. B. (2008). *A Guide to the Good Life: The Ancient Art of Stoic Joy* (1st edition). Oxford University Press.

Jung, C. G. (1981). *The Archetypes and The Collective Unconscious* (R. F. C. Hull, Trans.; 2nd edition). Princeton University Press.

Kant, I. (2009). *The Critique of Practical Reason* (null edition). CreateSpace Independent Publishing Platform.

Kant, I. (2018). *Groundwork for the Metaphysics of Morals: With an Updated Translation, Introduction, and Notes* (A. W. Wood, Ed.; Annotated edition). Yale University Press.

Laertius, D. (1925). *Diogenes Laertius: Lives of Eminent Philosophers,*

Volume I, Books 1-5 (R. D. Hicks, Trans.). Harvard University Press.

Martin, R. L. (2022). *A New Way to Think: Your Guide to Superior Management Effectiveness* (1st edition). Harvard Business Review Press.

Mercier, P. (2009). *Night Train To Lisbon* (Main edition). Atlantic Books.

Mill, J. S. (2015). *On Liberty, Utilitarianism and Other Essays* (M. Philp & F. Rosen, Eds.; Second edition). Oxford University Press.

Norman, J. (2018). *Adam Smith: Father of Economics*. Basic Books.

Plato. (2007). *Six Great Dialogues: Apology, Crito, Phaedo, Phaedrus, Symposium, The Republic* (B. Jowett, Trans.; 1st edition). Dover Publications.

Plato. (2020). *Euthyphro* (B. Jowett, Trans.). Independently published.

Rubin, R. (2023). *The Creative Act: A Way of Being*. Penguin Press.

Rumelt, R. (2017). *Good Strategy/Bad Strategy: The difference and why it matters* (Main edition). Profile Books.

Sartre, J.-P. (n.d.). *Nausea*.

Semler, R. (1995). *Maverick: The Success Story Behind the World's Most Unusual Workplace* (Reprint edition). Grand Central Publishing.

Storr, W. (2021). *The Science of Storytelling: Why Stories Make Us Human and How to Tell Them Better*. Harry N. Abrams.

Taleb, N. N. (2014). *Antifragile: Things That Gain from Disorder* (Reprint edition). Random House Publishing Group.

Voss, C. (2016). *Never Split the Difference: Negotiating As If Your Life Depended On It* (1st edition). Harper Business.

Warburton, N. (2012). *A Little History of Philosophy*. Yale University Press.

Willink, L. B. J. (2019). *The Dichotomy of Leadership*. St. Martin's Press.

Acknowledgments

Writing this book has been a fun experience for me. It provided me with the opportunity to bring forth and crystallize many of the concepts and ideas I had been practicing and tinkering with over the past few years.

I've had countless conversations and interactions with numerous people who helped me refine my thoughts. I'm especially grateful to those who graciously agreed to participate in my interviews. Thanks to them, I managed to understand some of the main concerns that professionals and business leaders face on a daily basis. Their insights significantly improved the content and structure of this work. I want to extend my heartfelt thanks to all those who participated or played a role in the realization of this project. Without you, it would not have materialized.

I want to also thank my wife, Vanina, who supported me during the months I spent writing and editing this book. She has been my interlocutor, playing a Socratic role, asking me questions, urging me to examine my assumptions, and suggesting new ideas to improve the content of the book and make it more engaging. She often helps me snap out of the vicious philosophical circle when I tend to overthink and complicate things beyond the necessary. Her feedback has been extremely helpful.

Over the past few years, I've had the chance to forge new bonds with those who signed up for my classes. Over time, I had the opportunity to meet many of them in person, both in Lebanon and in Spain. They have been great companions with whom I've had endless chats about philosophy, politics, food, and life in general. I'm extremely thankful for their ongoing assistance and feedback.

One person who has been especially pivotal, perhaps inadvertently, in helping me develop the ideas of the present work, is Oussama Himani. Over the past few years, we have established a nice rapport. He is well-read, and his interests range from art, business, philosophy, politics, and anywhere in between. A little over a year ago, he suggested I should read a book by Scott Hartley titled "The Fuzzy and the Techie." It acted as an inflection point for me. It was thanks to it that I went down the rabbit hole of a long list of interesting books that opened up a whole new world to me. Discussing this and other books with Oussama has also been crucial. It was thanks to him that I managed to articulate the difference between assumptions and conclusions. "My issue is not with other people's conclusions. I know my conclusions make sense and so do theirs. The problem is that oftentimes the assumptions we start from are wrong," he once said. This stuck with me.

I want to thank Rudi, David, and Telmo for their sustained encouragement and motivation. They always provide a fresh, well-thought-out, and interesting perspective on the topics discussed. They were also kind enough to read an early draft of the book and share their impressions.

This list of people I want to express my appreciation to is endless. I want to especially acknowledge each and every person who signed up for or promoted my philosophy courses. Your persistent backing means a lot to me. Without your trust and unwavering support, I would not have been able to sustain this venture. Special thanks go to Nassim Nicholas Taleb, Daniel Vassallo, and Dan Azzi for their generous endorsements and social media promotion. Their sustained encouragement, along with that of many others, enabled me to reach a broader audience, resulting in more enrollments in my courses.

I would also like to thank, again, each and every person who agreed to sit with me to chat about the ideas that figure in the book, including Abdallah, Anne Albert, Barry O'Reilly, Carla, Chris Wong, Costas Papaikonomou, Daniel Vassallo, David Wood, Dorie Clark, Edu, Elie Baroud, Gregory Sadler, Georg Meyer, Haifa, Hassan Osman, Henry Wyneken, Inês Pedro, Jamal El Kuweiss, Javi Rodriguez, Jim O'Shaughnessy, Johannes, John Stoszkowski, Louie Bacaj, Luca Dellana, Mariam S., Matt D. Plunkett, Megan Preston, Michael McGill, Monette M. Saade, Nahla Issa, Nicolas El-Helou, Nicola Rebagliati, Oussama Himani, Peter Askew, Philippe Caponis, Prab Randhawa, Rami Riman, Rani Arnaout, Robert Jamhouri, Robert Muir, Rudi Pawlitschko, Santiago Iñiguez, Sarah Ghanimeh, Sarah Mayyas, Sarah Yammine, Shane Breslin, Sheril Mathews, Shrief, Souhad Abu Zaki, Tanya Moushi, Tariq, Telmo Pires, Urtats, Utkarsh Amitabh, Vanina Lacoste, Vicente, Vikhyat, Walid Sinno, Xinran Ma, and Yahya Hajj Shehadeh. I had a great time learning from all of you. As I said, the list is long, so I'm extremely sorry if I missed anyone!

I also want to thank my parents and my brother, who have provided me with unconditional support in my recent endeavors. They have always been there when I most needed them.

And a huge thank you to Anthony Smyrski for the wonderful book cover design, and credits to Luis F. Lorenzo for the superb headshot.

About the Author

Mahmoud Rasmi is an independent writer, researcher, lecturer, and consultant. Over the past few years, he has been teaching philosophy to professionals and philosophy enthusiasts in a non-academic setting. He spent seven years as a university professor before he decided to venture into bringing philosophy back to the marketplace. He holds a PhD in Philosophy, and a BBA in Banking and Finance.

You can connect with me on:
- https://mahmoudrasmi.com
- https://x.com/Decafquest

Subscribe to my newsletter:
- https://decafquest.substack.com

Printed in Great Britain
by Amazon